MW00581219

Psychological Warfare and Deception

What You Need to Know about Human Behavior, Dark Psychology, Propaganda, Negotiation, Manipulation, and Persuasion

Contents

Part 1: Psychological Warfare

The Ultimate Guide to Understanding Human Behavior, Brainwashing, Propaganda, Deception, Negotiation, Dark Psychology, and Manipulation

Introduction

Does psychological warfare sound like something out of a James Bond novel? It could never affect you, could it? The truth is we all encounter some form of psychological warfare daily. This book is packed with easy to understand, jargon free ways to recognize the people who are trying to mess with your mind. If you want a comprehensive guide to stop being manipulated by the media, by your boss, or even by your partner, then look no further.

Expert advice doesn't have to be complicated and difficult to understand. *Psychological Warfare: The Ultimate Guide to Understanding Human Behavior, Brainwashing, Propaganda, Deception, Negotiation, Dark Psychology, and Manipulation* contains methods and exercises for everyone. Even if you are unaware of any form of manipulation or deception around you, it is worth knowing what potential dangers may arise in the future.

Chapter 1: What is Psychological Warfare?

Psychological warfare is known by a variety of names: PSYWAR, political warfare, "Hearts and Minds," PSYOP, and propaganda, to name a few. While most people are aware of the emergence of PSYWAR in the Second World War, it has much older origins and can be traced back as far as mankind itself.

Psychological warfare is the use of non-combat techniques to mislead and intimidate opponents and influence their psychological makeup. The techniques employed are designed to target thoughts, emotions, and attitudes with propaganda and threats to influence a person's actions.

Propaganda is not a threatening concept when used alone. Daniel Lerner wrote about the theory of "black," "white," and "gray" propaganda in his 1949 book *Sykewar; Psychological Warfare Against Germany, D-Day to V-E Day.*

• **White propaganda:** this defines the use of truthful information with a moderate bias to influence opponents. In the Second World War, this included millions of leaflets being dropped from planes over friendly and enemy territory. The leaflets stated their source and contained information designed to encourage support and contributions from the target audience.

• **Gray propaganda:** this will often be anonymous and contain information that is mainly true. If there are untrue statements, it is unlikely that they can be disproven. It involves presenting legitimate arguments that are free from agenda but have undefined sources.

• **Black propaganda:** put simply, fake news. This type of propaganda can contain both true and false statements, but it will appear to be legitimately sourced. This type of propaganda is designed to be wholly believable and is distributed with the intent of subversion.

The difference between gray and black propaganda is often a fine line. The most effective form of black propaganda is formed to look like it has come from trusted sources. Often the biggest giveaway is any links to gray propaganda that are less convincing.

There are many different forms of psychological warfare, but the result is just the same. The tactics employed are designed to demoralize, influence beliefs, change motives, and stir emotions. The targets of these tactics can range from the man on the street to the highest form of government, with everyone in between included.

Simple Forms of PSYOP

• **Word of mouth:** face to face communication may seem to be trustworthy, but it can be affected by rumors and mistruths.

• **Entertainment media sources:** we may feel that television and film are purely used for entertainment, but we can be influenced by them without knowing. Subtle messages and information can be presented in a way that seems like harmless fun, but it can be an effective way of altering people's thoughts and beliefs.

• **Audio media:** if you listen to the radio, you will already be aware of the power of sound. Gentle background noise can filter through and register quite easily. Even though you may be concentrating on other things, your brain is hard-wired to register sound.

• **Visual media**: leaflets, newspapers, and magazines may seem old fashioned, but they still play a role in PYSOP. They use visual images to appeal to our base instincts and influence our thoughts.

• **Online sources**: of course, the internet and online influences cannot be ignored. As we spend more time looking at screens, the chance to influence our thoughts increases.

Understanding psychological warfare means understanding its role in battle, the quintessential arena for enemies, and conflict.

Typical Tactics of PSYOP

• **Printed leaflets:** using printed leaflets to suggest the enemy should withdraw from the battlefield. Distributing simple leaflets with a strong message that surrender is their only choice will plant seeds of doubt within tired and battle-weary combatants. Instructions on how to surrender safely will often be accompanied by an assurance that no harm will come to them.

• **Overkill:** the enemy can often be convinced of their weaknesses by witnessing a massive attack from the opposing side. Employing a vast number of troops with advanced weaponry will often result in low morale and feelings of defeat for the other side.

• **Sleep deprivation:** this simple yet effective method involves projecting loud annoying sounds or rock music into the enemy's camp. This leads to a lack of sleep, which renders the troops ineffective and lackluster.

• **Enhanced rumors:** if the enemy believes you have advanced weapons that are chemical or biological, it can be just as effective as having them. Creating a perceived threat that has devastating effects will make them rethink their strategies.

• **"False flag" events:** if one side can convince its enemy that it has allies, this can be a turning point in any war or battle. Creating events and attacks that appear to have been carried out by fresh combatants can make the enemy feel overwhelmed and defeated.

Early Examples of Psychological Warfare

Since prehistoric times humans have understood the importance of gaining the upper hand in battle, by deploying some ingenious methods to lower the enemy's morale and weaken their spirits.

• **The Aztec death whistles:** in the late 1990s, archaeologists unearthed two skull-shaped instruments in Mexico. A temple dedicated to the wind god revealed the skeleton of a sacrificed man clutching the two objects. They were identified as "death whistles" often used to intimidate the enemy in battle. Reported to have sounded like the "scream of a thousand corpses," the whistles were used to unnerve the enemy and break their resolve.

• **Sacred shields:** in 525 BC, Emperor Cambyses II of Persia used the Egyptians' love of cats to defeat them at the Battle of Pelusium. The front line of the Persian soldiers included dogs, cats, and sheep as hostages. It is also reported that soldiers drew cats on their shields and pinned real cats to their armor. All these animals were revered by the Egyptians, which made them hesitate to attack.

• **Visual terror of Timur:** in the 14th century, the Muslim world and parts of Asia were ruled by Tamerlane, also known as "Timur the lame", a leader that was crippled by paralysis. It is reported that he beheaded his enemies and used their skills to build pyramids. Tamerlane is credited with some of the most effective terror tactics witnessed by the ancient world. Following his triumph over the Ottoman Empire, he locked the sultan in a cage and displayed him in his living quarters.

• **Vlad the Impaler:** often thought to be the inspiration for Bram Stoker's character "Dracula", Vlad the Impaler understood the importance of psychological warfare as far back as the 15th century. He was often faced with forces that were larger and more powerful than his own, but he knew how to fight with limited resources. Impaling corpses on spikes proved an effective way of striking terror into even the most formidable opponents.

- **Genghis Khan**: one of the most effective exponents of psychological warfare, Khan understood how to use misinformation to fool his enemies. He exaggerated the size of his forces and used horse-mounted dummies to reinforce the effect. He employed kettledrums to shatter his opponent's eardrums and prevent them from sleeping. He had spies in all camps and without fail knew more about his opponents than his enemies did of him. The Mongols became a mythical force that was prepared to kill huge numbers of troops and civilians alike.

Modern Use of Psychological Warfare

The first significant use of PSYOPS in the 20th century occurred during WWI. By the time the war was underway, it was quickly understood that tactics could be used to make the rest of the world more sympathetic to the British. Britain had a strong network that was used to create cross-cultural communications to succeed in the battle for good relations.

Britain also had an extensive diplomatic service that had previously worked with other nations successfully. The Germans, however, had previously tried to incite revolutions in various parts of the world that led to opinion becoming unfavorable.

Early in the war, A Propaganda Agency was formed that included some of the literary greats of the age. Luminaries, including Rudyard Kipling, Thomas Hardy, and other noteworthy authors, composed several publications to convince the world that Britain was the "good guys." The pamphlets listed atrocities committed against ordinary citizens by the German forces and were illustrated with emotionally charged images to support the information. These leaflets were distributed across neutral territories to encourage nations to join them in their struggle.

Later in the conflict, the agency changed tack. It concentrated on targeting the German troops who had spent many long years in atrocious conditions in the trenches. The leaflets were designed to look as if prisoners of war held in Britain had written them. It portrayed a vision of humane conditions, good food, and clean clothes. It urged the soldiers to surrender and told stories of the German hierarchy eating well and living the high life. It is thought that over 25 million of these leaflets were printed and distributed throughout the conflict.

The British were not alone in employing these tactics. French leaders took control of the nation's media and used it to create articles and leaflets that berated the German forces and government. France worked hand in hand with their European counterparts to create bad feelings toward the German forces. It is believed that the Germans discovered the power of PSYOPS a lot later. They succeeded in creating good feelings by giving Lenin, a Russian revolutionary, free travel on a secure train following the defeat of the Tzar. This action led to Russia withdrawing from the war soon after.

PSYOPS Used in WWII

Just a few decades later, the world was once again in conflict. Throughout the war, the Axis and the Allies engaged in prolonged use of propaganda aimed at the psychological manipulation of the enemy. No longer was war a test of superior weaponry and armed troops. It involved the manipulation of the worst and most vulnerable parts of the human psyche to systematically reduce soldiers to their knees until they were too demoralized to fight.

Leaflets depicting marital infidelity and images of families being torn apart by the war were distributed. These were designed to increase the insecurity felt by soldiers who had wives and loved ones back home. Hitler first introduced the use of trained psychologists to aid his war efforts, but Britain was quick to join in the race for psychological dominance.

The science of combat psychiatry emerged, and the psychological effects of warfare on the individual were listed for the first time.

It was discovered that the stresses of war consist of five different stages which are:

1) Pain.

2) Cold.

3) Hunger and thirst.

4) Fatigue.

5) Boredom and loneliness.

Initially, troops are gung-ho about going into battle and filled with nervous enthusiasm. As they enter the combat zone, there is a sense of resignation. They begin to feel a sense of their own mortality and become depressed. They are in a strange place, surrounded by the noise and the smells of the battlefield. As the process continues, they begin to think about family back home. The environment they are facing day in and day out becomes overwhelming, and they sink further into depression. This is when they are vulnerable to psychological warfare, and both combatants realized this early in the conflict.

Radio propaganda emerged from all sides accompanied by printed leaflets, newspapers, and news sheets. The Allies used motion pictures, emotionally charged images, and radio campaigns to infiltrate the enemy home fronts.

As the US entered the conflict, the propaganda level was raised considerably. The Japanese were also adept at PSYOPS, and every campaign in the Pacific theater was enhanced by a form of PSYOPS on both sides.

Possibly the most controversial form of psychological warfare was the bombing of Pearl Harbor in Hawaii by the Japanese. The attack was designed to demoralize the US and make them leave the conflict. The Japanese thought that such a bold move would make the US back off and leave the Allies to fight alone. This was possibly the biggest mistake of the whole conflict. The attack awakened the fighting spirit of the US and led to a sweeping campaign that targeted the Pacific Islands. The bombing of Hiroshima and Nagasaki finally brought the curtain down on the war and saw the Allies emerge triumphantly.

Iraq and the Weapons of Mass Destruction

More recently, the citizens of the US and the UK were subjected to a campaign of misinformation, stating that Iraq held "weapons of mass destruction." This led to the invasion of Iraq, based on "evidence" apparently held by the Governments of both countries. This information came from the highest level of government in both nations, and the call for war seemed inevitable.

This form of PSYOPS is used to manipulate the public into supporting governmental policies that would otherwise be repellant. Did the government genuinely believe that these weapons existed, or did they use the claim to manipulate the public?

PSYOPS in Everyday Life

The actions we take and the words we speak will always affect other people to some extent. But are we subject to a higher level of psychological manipulation? The simple answer is *yes*.

Take advertising. The images you see, and the products you view are all carefully placed to encourage you to buy. Attractive people are used to make you want the life or belongings they are advertising. By using models to market a product, you are led to believe you will appear more attractive when you buy that particular product.

Assertive language is used by advertisers and the media to encourage people to conform. They use phrases designed to make the customer feel better about themselves. Using "assertive language" involves being both persuasive and empathetic at the same time.

A workplace is also a place where psychological methods will be used to manipulate you. This is not always a bad thing. A great manager will be able to use psychological conditioning to encourage team members and get the best from them. Bad managers will use aggressive forms of manipulation that can result in the opposite effect.

The truth is that psychological triggers surround us. This should not make us nervous or paranoid, but we should be aware that manipulation is part of our daily lives. Learn how to spot truthful information and discount the manufactured information presented to you.

Chapter 2: It All Starts with Dark Personalities

Now we delve into the world of human personalities. Our behavior and personalities are what shape us as human beings, and people exhibiting dark personality traits have been described as part of the "Dark Triad." This is a term coined by psychologists for people who are prone to manipulating and deceiving others to get their own way.

The Dark Triad is a term used to describe the three personality traits that indicate a "dark" personality.

Three Personality Traits

1) Narcissism. Some of the less obvious signs of a narcissist are:

- They are likable: classic narcissists will give a great first impression. They are confident and charismatic.

- They will be found in leadership roles: that is not to say that they make good leaders, but they will be happier to take on the role. Narcissists will be more self-possessed and, therefore, more likely to apply for promotions.

- They always manage to turn the conversation toward themselves: it wouldn't matter if you had the most exciting news ever, within minutes, the conversation will be about them.

- They refuse to take the blame: when a narcissist is talking about themselves, it will normally be about their successes and triumphs. Even when the story involves failure, it will never be the narcissist's fault.

- They love to look good: narcissists will make the most of their appearance and will be well-groomed. This doesn't mean that all attractive people or those who take pride in their appearance are narcissists.

- They surround themselves with the best: material items are very important to narcissists, and they love to display them. One example of narcissism is the person who drives up in a Maserati, yet tells you what a great deal they got on the price!

- Media presence: how they appear to others is ultra-important to narcissists. They will be aware of every image on their social media, and it will not contain a single bad picture. They will have a wide range of friends and spend lots of time maintaining their online presence.

- Everything is personal: a narcissist will not welcome any form of criticism. It will be an affront to their self-image, and they will not react well.

- They struggle to keep relationships: narcissists are constantly looking to improve the person they are with and so are more likely to cheat. They will have a history of failed relationships and infidelity.

2) Machiavellianism. The common traits of this personality disorder are:

- Self-focus: they are solely focused on their own ambitions and interests.

- They use flattery to win over others: they are so self-assured that even the most blatant lies can be interpreted as flattery. They persuade other people that they admire them and find them special.

- Can come across as difficult to engage: when talking to someone, they will often be distracted by other conversations or events. This is because they believe that everyone else is below them and that there is something more interesting elsewhere.

- They lie effortlessly: their moral compass is totally skewed. They believe that the end justifies the means, and any lie they tell is perfectly acceptable.

- They lack morals and principles: normal social conventions are for mugs. They believe they have a given right to behave within their own personal moral boundaries.

- Lack of empathy: they fail to understand that other people matter or that their actions affect other people emotionally. People with Machiavellian traits will be unable to show sympathy or remorse. They can't connect with people or comfort them when needed.

- Failure to maintain relationships: nobody is good enough for them, so they are constantly seeking to improve their partner.

- Prone to casual sexual encounters without guilt: they don't believe that infidelity is wrong. They simply see an opportunity to have sex with someone as self-satisfying and gratifying. They will cheat on partners regularly, and this is part of the reason they are unable to maintain relationships.

- Can display high levels of patience: their calculating nature means that they see opportunity with every encounter. This means that they can be more willing to show patience with people or situations that may prove valuable to them in the future.

- Prioritize material objects over personal relationships: the big house and the flash car will be much more important to them than a loving partner or happy family. Machiavellian people are all about the impression they give to others and how people perceive them.

Put quite simply, Machiavellian personalities are selfish, self-obsessed, and quite unaware of the needs of others.

3) **Psychopathy.** The common traits of a psychopath are:

- An enhanced sense of self-importance: even the smallest throwaway compliment will serve to inflate their ego.

- Requires constant stimulation: psychopaths are notoriously hard to engage. They will find quite calming situations difficult to maintain. They are constantly looking for the next moment of danger or excitement.

- Never says sorry: they believe that all their actions are justified, so why would they need to apologize. They are completely unaware of other people's emotions or feelings.

- Lack of remorse: in the mind of the psychopath, once an action is committed, it becomes redundant. They are immediately seeking the next thrill or emotional high. When their actions are questioned, they genuinely can't summon up remorse. They have no concept of contrition.

- Promiscuous sex life: sex provides them with a bolt of adrenaline, so they are constantly looking for sexual encounters. Psychopaths will often try sex with partners from both sexes as it is less about the physical encounter but more about the boost to their ego. They will seek encounters that provide them with danger and excitement.

• Lack of emotion: they have no emotions but can be adept at faking them. They understand the importance that other people place in emotional displays and can be convincing when required.

• Lack of restraint: part of the lack of emotion is an overwhelming absence of fear. If you have no fear, then boundaries are lowered. Why would you not do something if you don't fear it?

• They believe the world owes them a living: they are adept at using charm, flattery, and manipulation to mold people to their will. This will get them a level of success without actually working on a normal level. If they can see a way to improve their own circumstances, they will take it, no matter how it affects others.

• Short term goals and ambitions: they see no point in planning for the future because it is a concept they don't grasp. Psychopaths live in the moment and don't understand long term goals or ambition.

• Prone to overindulgent bursts of temper or rage: if things aren't going their way, it can lead up to a level of stress that they react with violent repercussions. Even the slightest setback can seem devastating as they have no concept of failure and don't know how to deal with it.

• Can be charming when trying to influence others: they understand how to turn on the charm when required.

• Has a history of childhood behavioral problems: they will have been a "problem" child from adolescence? They may have a history of cruelty to other children and animals. Their parents will have found it impossible to control them or discipline them.

- Prone to petty crime: nothing is off bounds for a psychopath. Even the pettiest of crimes will give them a momentary thrill, and they will constantly be seeking that thrill.

In a perfect world, these traits would not be "normal" in successful people, but we all know the world is far from perfect. Narcissists are successful when choosing their mates, even though they lack the skills to form long term relationships. Machiavellian traits are also useful for social manipulation, and when combined with a narcissistic personality, it confers a marked advantage when dating.

The combination of the first two Dark Triad traits is also advantageous for those looking to enter the business world or to become active in politics. People with these traits will be naturally able to manipulate others and pursue their goals with ruthless ambition. They won't worry about who they upset on their journey to success. It is certainly true that those who have inner steel will find their path clears quicker than those with a conscience.

A report printed in the *Journal of Business Ethics* in 2016 stated that the three Dark Triad behaviors work together to allow people to act fraudulently without considering the consequences. In the report titled *The Effects of the Dark Triad on Unethical Behavior,* it was concluded that narcissism motivates individuals to indulge in behaviors that would be unethical to others. The Machiavellianism would then alter the perceptions of the acts and behaviors and give the perpetrator a misplaced sense of justice. Psychopathy would help them rationalize the behavior and remove all feelings of guilt or remorse.

The "D" Factors

Recently published research projects have defined a broader definition of the dark side of human personality. They have coined the phrase "the D factor" to cover some of the other personality traits that are indicative of a dark personality.

The Dark Triad has noticeable differences and can be found individually as well as simultaneously in people, but some other personality traits should be examined.

• **Spitefulness:** anyone who has used the phrase "to cut off one's nose to spite one's face" understands the common conception of spitefulness. It is the willingness to put yourself at the risk of harm to make sure other people suffer.

• **Moral disengagement:** the thought processes employed by a person are different from others and allows the person to behave without any negative emotions. They have no distress, guilt, or shame, even when they behave unethically.

• **Egoism:** not to be confused with egotism, egoism is the ethical theory based on the pursuit of self-interest. Egotism is the overstressing of an individual's worth.

• **Sadism:** the desire to cause pain for pleasure. Sadists believe that they are entitled to cause others pain and suffering, for their own pleasure.

The studies have shown a common factor between all dark personality traits. That is the tendency to place personal goals and interests above anything else. This common core proves a moral justification for distress, pain, and suffering caused to others without any form of emotional repercussions, like remorse. However, all dark personality factors are not the same, and they can result in varying actions and behavior.

How Are Dark Triad Traits Measured?

There are multiple ways to assess if someone has psychological traits that are defined by the Dark Triad. The most popular way is to test an individual with a personal inventory test, to explore the presence of these undesirable traits.

One of the most popular forms of this test was developed in 2010 when two psychologists from Florida collaborated to produce a twelve-question quiz that was nicknamed the "Dirty Dozen."

The questionnaire has four questions per trait. The first four relate to Machiavellianism, the middle four to psychopathy, and the final four to narcissism. The higher the score, the stronger the tendencies.

The first four questions address the individual's attitude to manipulation, flattery, exploitation, and deceit when trying to influence others. The middle four questions involve their attitude to cynicism, morality, remorse, and levels of callousness. The final four questions involve statements about themselves, their self-perception, how others view them, and the importance of prestige and status.

Participants are asked to rate statements with a mark that indicates the relevance they feel the statement holds. The higher the mark, the higher the Dark Triad tendencies. There are multiple tests available online, some are more elaborate, and some are simpler. If you really want to discover just how dark your personality is, then they can give you an indication. Providing you answer honestly, of course!

While the police and law enforcement agencies regularly use these tests to establish the personality traits of suspects, can they prove a helpful aid for other agencies who need to know who they are dealing with?

The military, for instance, has unearthed some interesting data about the presence of the Dark Triad traits in their personnel. The scientific community studied the occurrence of these traits in personnel who carried out war crimes while serving in the military and found a cluster of examples. In both the Iraq and Afghanistan conflicts, there were examples of soldiers carrying out atrocities on civilians while serving in the countries. The systematic abuse of prisoners has been a recurring problem in the military and displays a likelihood that some soldiers have an inner core of darkness.

Of course, it can be argued that anyone who voluntarily signs up for a job that will involve fighting and/or killing other people must have a special set of skills. This is apparent, especially in the military, as the elite soldiers will often present with dark traits. They have the aggression and lack of moral restraint to get the job done— no matter what the consequences. The theatre of war is not the place for regular rules and restrictions, and sometimes personnel with these dark traits are essential for success.

It has been suggested that more stringent testing is required to stop incidents of war crimes and unacceptable behavior. However, there is also research that suggests that military training of cadets is designed to make them more socially dominant and aggressive. Developing a healthy balance is the obvious aim, but improving the standard of military ethics may eliminate some much-needed darker traits that are part of a successful soldier.

So, what can we deduce from the Dark Triad personality types? People with these traits will often initially be successful and reap the rewards from their self-confident approach, coupled with a lack of morals. However, under long term scrutiny, they will be found out. There will be situations of fraud, outright lying, cheating, and general disrepute. It is inevitable we will all have some contact with people who have dark personality traits, and we may even find them charming at first. Recognizing when to cut ties could save you a ton of heartache and give you peace of mind.

Bear in mind that most psychopaths and other Dark Triad personalities make a good first impression. Try and scratch the surface as soon as you can and see what lies under that charming, glossy exterior. You may find a darker underbelly that could become dangerous to you and your sanity.

Chapter 3: The Art of Deception

If somebody tells you that they have never told a lie, then the truth is that they are a liar. While most people are generally honest, the average person lies at least once a day. Deception is a common form of communication, and we all engage in it. Some lies are huge, while others are deployed to make situations better or to spare someone's feelings.

The truth is that it is difficult to avoid lying. We do it to get what we want. We do it to avoid embarrassing situations. We do it to cover up our mistakes etc. etc. and deception can be a difficult habit to break. However, if you are caught in a lie, it can be destructive. Other people will feel cheated and disappointed by your lies. They will distance themselves from you and encourage others to mistrust you. If you tell the truth whenever possible, you can avoid this social void and lead a happier life.

How to Recognize an Effective Liar

Deception, duplicity, fraudulence, chicanery, and deviousness are the bedrock of a Dark Triad personality. They are adept in social situations and can lie shamelessly.

Here are some other ways to spot an adept liar:

• They are natural performers: think about actors and the job they do. Actors "pretend" to be someone else for a living. They are professional liars. If you are in the company of someone who appears to be performing and talking to an audience, then your radar should be beeping.

• They are manipulative: successful liars can steer conversations and situations to suit their agenda. If a subject crops up that makes them uncomfortable, they will have a strategy to change the subject quickly but without any awkwardness.

• Expressive and attractive: it may seem unfair, but attractive people are trusted more than their less attractive peers. Combine attraction with an animated way of speaking, and you have the perfect storm for a believable liar. Of course, not all pretty people are liars, but try and remember to be more aware when confronted with an attractive and animated person.

• Eloquence: stumbling over your words or filling the conversation with verbal pauses like "hmm" or "uh" is less engaging. An effective liar will avoid meaningless phrases like "you know" or "it's like," as eloquence is more convincing.

• Good recall: liars are often caught out by memory loss. Inconsistencies in a story are the biggest clue when trying to spot a lie.

• Keeping information concealed: when confronted by a pointed question, a seasoned liar will be frugal with details. They will skirt the details and say as little as possible. Using phrases like "I truly can't remember" or "I have no clear recollections" are designed to avoid the need for a constructed lie.

• They will constantly be trying to prove their honesty: honest people don't need to convince you they are honest and will state their facts and information without back up. When someone is lying to you, they may feel the need to assure you of their "honest" intentions. Phrases like "I swear that is true" or "to be perfectly honest" should set alarm bells ringing. If they are emphatic about their honesty, the chances are, they are being dishonest or lying.

• Rehearsed answers: when you ask an honest person a question, they will pause and consider their response. The pause may be just a second or so, but it can tell you volumes. Liars have a script and will have rehearsed their answers beforehand. If someone answers you immediately with an answer that is full of detail and smoothly executed, it could be a lie. Most people would expect liars to be hesitant and unprepared for on the spot questions, when actually the opposite can be true. If you ask someone what they did on holiday last year, honest people will have to take a moment to remember. Slick, polished responses are a giveaway sign of dishonesty.

• Listen for pronouns: liars are constantly trying to distance themselves from their lies. They will avoid using the pronouns "I," "me," and "myself" in conversation. They will refer to themselves in the third person instead. In writing, the most common point of view is often the third person, so the use of it by storytellers is well documented. This makes a lot of sense, as liars are essentially telling you a story, so recognizing this type of speech can be a classic way of identifying a lie.

• Tone and structure: listening to someone's voice can be a great way to spot a lie or liar. When people tell a lie, there can be a slight change in the tone of their voice and how they form sentences. Listen for a higher tone of voice or a lowering of tone. If a person's rate of speech alters, it may mean they are less than truthful. Honest people speak with a constant, measured tone as they have nothing to hide. When the brain is working in overdrive to think up different ways of constructing fresh information, it can forget to regulate speech patterns and tone of voice.

The Body Language of a Liar

The signs someone is lying to you can be difficult to spot, especially if they are a practiced liar. There are no tried and tested ways to determine whether someone is lying with 100% certainty, but there are some signs to watch out for. Verbal clues are important, but body language can tell us even more. How a person reacts to a situation will be harder to control and can give us major clues when someone is lying. Body language accounts for 55% of our perception when communicating with other people.

So, what do we need to look for?

Quick Changes in the Position of Their Head

If you see someone jerking their head right before they answer a question, it could be an indication; they are not truthful. Bowing their head or cocking it to one side is a sure sign that something is amiss. Any sudden movement of the head should be recognized as a potential warning sign that the person is lying.

A Change in Breathing

When you lie, you put pressure on your body, and it will tense up. When people lie, they are both tense and nervous, so this will affect their normal heart rate. It will become elevated, and this, in turn, increases the flow of blood. This will cause the shoulders to become tense and rise from their normal position and cause the person's voice to become shallow. In essence, they are experiencing sensations related to being out of breath, which will change their breathing patterns.

Blushing and Sweating

The symptoms above will also result in a rise in temperature, which could result in red cheeks and a heightened complexion. Sweat on the upper lip is a sure sign of anxiety, as are sweaty palms. Any sign of an increase in temperature without external cause could be a sign of lying.

Lack of Movement

It is a common misconception that people who are lying will fidget. Twitching and nervous movement can just indicate a level of anxiety that is normal. In fact, a lack of movement is a far greater sign that something isn't right. The human body is primed with a fight or flight response, and standing still is the first stage of the fight response.

The body is readying itself for confrontation and will be conserving energy for the up and coming fight. When people speak and engage with others, it is normal to move the body with subtle, relaxed, and mostly unconscious movements. A lack of movement, which leads to a form of catatonic and rigid stance, is a sure sign they are readying themselves for an argument.

They May Touch or Cover Their Mouth

This has been proved to be one of the most telling signs that someone is lying to you. Covering the mouth with a hand is an automatic response to untruths or confrontations. When adults raise their hands and place them in front of their lips or mouth, they are indicating a disengagement from communications. They may be unaware they are making the gesture and carry on the conversation, but you should be warned that their words may contain a measure of untruths.

They May Cover Vulnerable Body Parts

The throat, chest, abdomen, and head are all vulnerable parts of the body. The soft skin in these areas is particularly at danger when under attack. The covering of these areas with a hand indicates a level of attack or fear. This may not apply to liars as such, but it does indicate you have touched a nerve with something you have said. When you are in conversation with people, watch for this telling gesture that will indicate you are causing them concern.

Shuffling of the Feet

A quick look at someone's feet can tell you a lot. We have already touched on the fight or flight response that humans are naturally born with. While the rest of the body may be preparing to fight, shuffling feet are another indication of a potential liar. They are uncomfortable with the situation and are eager to get away.

The Inability to Speak

The automatic nervous system is prone to stress when you lie, and it will cause the saliva in your mouth to dry up. This, in turn, causes the mucous membrane to become dry and fail to work correctly. Watching someone trying to speak and failing can mean this process is heightened. Biting the lip and pursing of the mouth are also unconscious attempts to generate saliva by other means.

Eye Contact

We understand people who fail to maintain eye contact can be viewed as shady. They must have something to hide, right? While this is true, there is another side to the coin. Practiced liars will overcompensate by maintaining an unnatural amount of eye contact. They will use a cold hard stare to try and intimidate you and will often be the last to break contact. Honest people having a natural conversation will occasionally break eye contact and then reengage. This is normal behavior, but liars will try and use a steely gaze to control and manipulate you.

This type of contact can lead to the eyes drying out. Watch for rapid blinking, as this indicates an effort to rehydrate the eyes without breaking contact.

They Will Use Aggressive Gestures

If a liar feels like they are being confronted or are about to get called out, they will attempt to turn the tables with aggression. Pointing at things, thrusting the chin out, and sweeping movements of the arms are all an indication you are getting under their skin.

Their face may still be maintaining a measured, calm expression, but any sign of aggression is a sure sign they are getting stressed.

What Are the Different Types of Deception?

The most common form of deception is a direct statement that is not true. Then you have the liars who distort facts to make them appear true. Leaving information out is regarded as the sin of omission. Self-serving lies are all about getting what you want, making yourself look better, and covering up any mistakes. Some people use these types of lies to increase their feelings of self-worth and confidence.

Could I Be Lying to Myself?

Most certainly. Lying is not just an outward-facing process. The lies people tell themselves fall into two different categories. If you are inflating your self-esteem with lies, then you run the risk of failing to address the issues you are facing. This can lead to serious feelings of delusion that can spiral out of control.

On the other hand, there is the thought that lying to yourself about your limits can be a positive way of thinking. Think about it, when you imagine yourself achieving accomplishments that deep down you are far from certain are possible, is this a lie, or is it just a positive mental attitude? Lies are not always black and white, and they will never be totally eradicated from the human psyche.

When considering psychological warfare and the manipulation of others, it is important to understand certain forms of deception. Gaslighting is one of these tactics that falls into the category of ultimate dirty fighting. It is a tactic in which a person or entity makes their victim question every aspect of their being. They manipulate their victims over a period of time until they have total control. It is a form of brainwashing that has been used for centuries and is still alive and well in modern times.

The technique has been used by dictators, cult leaders, and abusers, and can be directed at individuals or groups of people.

So, how well do you think your "BS detector" is working? Can you spot a liar within minutes? The truth is that most of us are confronted with so many lies daily; we have lost the ability to detect deception. The information above should have given you the ability to become a real-life lie spotter. So, here's a test to see what your lie quotient is, your "lie-Q" if you like.

These Twenty Questions Will Assess Your Lie-Q:

1) Which response indicates the highest level of dishonesty?

    a) "To be honest ..."

    b) "To be brutally honest ..."

    c) "Honestly ..."

2) How do you recognize a fake smile?

    a) Lack of action in the muscles around the eyes.

    b) Lack of action in the muscles around the mouth.

    c) Lack of action in the muscles around the jaw.

3) When someone is telling a lie, they will blink rapidly:

    a) True.

    b) False.

    c) Probably.

4) The use of strict chronology will be found in:

    a) A true story.

    b) A false story.

    c) Either type of story.

5) When asked a detailed question, will a dishonest person repeat any details?

    a) No.

    b) They will repeat key details.

    c) They will repeat the whole statement.

6) A deceptive person will avoid eye contact:

    a) Sometimes.

    b) True.

    c) False, they will use excessive eye contact instead.

7) Will a deceptive person answer a random question with a pause?

    a) Sometimes.

    b) Never.

    c) Always.

8) When someone is telling you a lie will they:

    a) Remain still.

    b) Move naturally.

    c) Become over-animated with their movements.

9) If you have caught someone out in a lie should you:

    a) Ask directly what made them lie.

    b) Keep quiet and let them talk.

    c) Ask them what they felt when they lied to you.

10) When someone is lying will you get the most clues from:

    a) Their words.

    b) Their nonverbal communication.

    c) A mixture of the two.

11) A practiced liar will use the following to make them seem viable:

    a) Expressive gestures.

    b) Grandiose statements.

    c) All of the above.

12) When someone covers their throat with their hand, it indicates:

    a) Sincerity.

    b) Lies.

    c) Fear.

13) Practiced liars will:

    a) Use personal pronouns.

    b) Will talk in the second person.

    c) Will use third-person pronouns.

14) If you are questioning someone and their eyes dart to the left, are they telling the truth?

    a) They are telling the truth.

    b) Unsure.

    c) They are lying.

15) If someone is giggling when they answer a question, does this mean they are lying?

    a) Always.

    b) Never.

    c) Sometimes.

16) Do liars use sarcasm?

    a) Always.

    b) Never.

    c) Sometimes.

17) When someone is lying their breathing will:

   a) Become faster.

   b) Slow down.

   c) Remain the same.

18) If someone is lying to a group of people will they place themselves:

   a) At the center of attention.

   b) On the outskirts of the group.

   c) In a place where they have limited interaction with the rest of the group.

19) Does a good liar believe the things they say?

   a) No.

   b) Sometimes.

   c) Yes.

20) Do liars do well in social situations?

   a) Sometimes.

   b) Always.

   c) Never.

While this is just a fun test, it should give you an idea of how switched on your "BS" meter is. Add up the points to see how you scored.

Answers

   1. a) = 3 b) = 5 c) = 1

   2. a) = 3 b) = 5 c) = 1

   3. a) = 5 b) = 1 c) = 3

   4. a) = 1 b) = 5 c) = 3

   5. a) = 1 b) = 3 c) = 5

   6. a) = 3 b) = 1 c) = 5

7. a) = 3 b) = 5 c) = 1

8. a) = 5 b) = 1 c) = 3

9. a) = 3 b) = 5 c) = 1

10. a) = 1 b) = 3 c) = 5

11. a) = 1 b) = 3 c) = 5

12. a) = 1 b) = 5 c) = 3

13. a) = 1 b) = 3 c) = 5

14. a) = 1 b) = 3 c) = 5

15. a) = 1 b) = 3 c) = 5

16. a) = 1 b) = 5 c) = 3

17. a) = 5 b) = 3 c) = 1

18. a) = 5 b) = 1 c) = 3

19. a) = 1 b) = 3 c) = 5

20. a) = 3 b) = 5 c) = 1

The Results Are as Follows

Under 35: oh dear, you are a trusting soul. Maybe you are one of the innocents of the world and you love the fact that you see the best in people. Life, however, will rear up and bite you on the ass. You need to realize there are some bad people out there and they will tell you lies. Maybe you aren't ready to be a cynical hardnosed member of society, but you do need to sharpen those instincts.

Between 35 and 70: this is the average *lie-Q* category. You understand that you are being lied to regularly, but you have the skills to weed out the really dangerous ones. You may get caught out in some situations, but you will survive!

Over 70: well, hello to the human lie detector! Nobody is getting the best of you any time soon. You can spot "BS" from the outset and won't be taken for a ride by anyone. You may want to rein it in a little, though, as you may come across as cold and cynical at times.

Chapter 4: Psychological Warfare in Relationships

In the following chapters, we will be discussing different tactics in psychological warfare in relationships and at work. One of the most devastating tactics used is known as "gaslighting." Before we delve into the different ways that gaslighting affects a relationship, it is important to understand the basic principles of the insidious process and how destructive it can be.

What Are Gaslighting Tactics?

1) The perpetrator tells outrageous lies. Imagine a lie so blatant being delivered with a straight face. They are setting a precedent. If they can conjure up such a huge lie from the onset, then what can you expect in the future? You are now off-balance and are unsure if anything they say is true.

2) The perpetrator uses complete denial no matter what the situation. When someone is gaslighting you, they will deny everything. Even if you catch them out in a lie, or hear them say something hurtful, they will look you in the eye and deny it. The more they do this, the more you doubt yourself.

3) The perpetrator will use emotional warfare to grind you down. Once they have established what is important to you, they will use this information to destroy you. They will denigrate the things that are the foundation of your being. If you are proud of anything in your life, they will attempt to make it worthless.

4) The perpetrator will slowly wear you down. One of the insidious things about gaslighting is it is done gradually. The perpetrator will take their time and chip away at your defenses with snide comments and lies every so often. They know how to introduce seeds of self-doubt and nourish them with derogatory comments.

5) The perpetrator will change tack and try to be positive. When someone has nothing good to say about you, there is a better chance you will recognize what they are trying to do. When they use positive statements to describe you, they make you question your judgment. This is all about making you rethink your every decision and conclude you imagine things.

6) The perpetrator projects their faults onto you. If you are in a relationship where your partner is cheating, they will often throw the same accusation back at you. This is a deflection tactic at its simplest. When you start to defend yourself, you are distracted from the gaslighter's aberrant behavior, and take your eye off the situation.

7) The perpetrator attracts a posse of "yes men," so-to-speak. Gaslighters recognize people who will stick by them no matter what they do. They will then turn to these people to reiterate their negative comments about you. Common comments such as "see, I told you your behavior was wrong, this person thinks so too," will be used to isolate you. The more people who agree with the gaslighter, the stronger they become. They will lower your defenses until you think they are the only person you can trust. This leads you right back to them, and the power is in their hands.

8) The perpetrator questions your sanity. We all have a fear of being seen as crazy or unhinged. A gaslighter will use the term to put you down personally and with other people. As you begin to question your sanity, you spiral into self-doubt.

Psychological warfare is not restricted to the battlefield or international conflicts. It surrounds us, and the only way to ensure you don't become a victim is to recognize the tactics.

Relationships form a key part of our lives and can be the most fulfilling, wonderful experiences. Even when relationships break up, you can be left with amazing memories and fondness for your former partner. In a perfect world, we would be able to have successful relationships with amicable breakups and move on to the next chapter of our lives.

Of course, we all know this is not a perfect world, and we will be subject to bad relationships, but what can we do about it?

Recognizing what is happening and dealing with it is the first step to understanding how to improve, heal, or simply walk away from troubled relationships.

Are you ready to empower yourself? Let's consider these classic forms of manipulation and how to deal with them:

1) **Bullying**: this is the least subtle and easiest to recognize form of manipulation. Your partner will use aggressive tactics to get their own way. For instance, they may ask you to drive them to work and pick them up after. While this may be a normal request, it is the tone of voice that needs to be addressed. Are you given a choice, or is the way in which you are asked threatening? If the latter is true, then you should consider how important this relationship is. Do you feel the aggression may escalate from verbal to physical violence? If the answer is "yes" or even "maybe," then get out immediately.

2) **Gaslighting**: if any of the gaslighting tactics listed above ring true, then leave straight away. If your partner is constantly trying to

mess with your mind and questioning your sanity, they are manipulating you in the worst possible way. This is abuse.

3) **Playing the victim**: do you find yourself apologizing even when you weren't in the wrong? Your partner is playing the victim. They're using emotional triggers to make you feel bad and to make themselves feel justified. If your partner refuses to take responsibility for their own actions, you must nip this behavior in the bud. Apologize for what *you* have done, but refuse to apologize for their bad behavior.

The best way to do this is to dissect the argument and say something like, "I apologize for becoming angry and raising my voice, but you upset me with your actions. You made me feel bad, and you should apologize for that." Hopefully, this will result in a frank discussion and will clear the air.

4) **Convenient neediness**: are you constantly taking up the reins in your relationship? Does your partner conveniently feel weak or have a headache when you need help with the housework? Do they suffer from anxiety when you want them to accompany you out to any special occasion? Yet when it is time to go to fun events, they seem to find the energy to go out and have a great time. Unless they have underlying health issues, they are manipulating you by making you feel sorry for them.

Do you really want a relationship with someone you pity? If you are staying in a relationship because you worry about what will happen to your partner if you leave, then this is not a healthy situation. Put yourself first and make plans to leave. If you can arrange a support system for your partner when you leave, it will help. Chances are they will be fine, but you will feel better.

5) **Nothing is free**: if you feel obligated to your partner whenever they do something for you, then they are manipulating you. In a healthy relationship, you should be able to give and receive gifts and favors without feeling there are strings attached. It is normal to do

cool things for each other, but there should be no compulsion to reciprocate.

6) Using your love as a tool to get what they want: do you hear the phrase "If you loved me you would ..." often? Does your partner preempt a request with this phrase? Do they use guilt and emotion to control your responses? If you say no to them, will they revert to statements of emotion to prod and shame you into compliance? If you hear "You would if you loved me," when you say "no" to something, then you need to shut it down.

Try a different method of communication. They may feel it is normal to bring your feelings into a conversation, but it isn't healthy to guilt your partner. Tell them to rein it in and word their requests differently. Tell them you will still take their request seriously, even without emotional manipulation.

You could say something like, "Even if I won't take the car to the garage, it doesn't mean I love you any less" or "I can still love you with all my being without doing everything you ask." Ask for a more direct form of communication and tell them to stop staking your relationship on the most mundane requests.

7) Emotional blackmail: this type of manipulation is ugly. It plays on your deepest feelings and makes you a hostage. When someone uses threats and dramatic statements to keep you from leaving, it plays on your basest emotions. When your partner tells you they will die if you leave or that they will kill themselves if you leave, they are blackmailing you.

You are being made to feel responsible for someone else's life, and that is not right. In a healthy relationship, you may feel a partial responsibility for your partner's happiness and well-being, and that's fine. However, you should never feel solely responsible for their life.

In these types of situations, the threats are just that. Empty threats designed to tie you to that person for as long as they want you to remain. They are taking any form of choice away from you and keeping you as an emotional hostage. You may be able to deal with this using couples therapy and counseling to find out why they are acting in this way. Or you could just leave. There is no reason to be cruel, and when your partner threatens to harm themselves, you can promise to get them medical help but distance yourself from any further actions. Tell them you can't deal with them when they threaten self-harm and walk away. It may seem harsh, but you need to stop feeling guilty or responsible.

8) **Overusing kindness as a weapon**: now, before you dismiss this type of manipulation offhand, try thinking about why your partner is kind to you. Are they using gifts and compliments to coerce you into doing something you don't want? We all know that the beginning of a relationship can be magical. You are both in the honeymoon period, and gifts will be a normal part of your courtship. However, if the gifts and compliments are over the top, consider if they are being used as a form of bribery.

Also, consider if any compliments they pay you have ulterior motives. For instance, if your partner is constantly telling you that you are wasted in your current job, and you should apply for a promotion or seek a better-paid position, there could be two reasons for this. The first reason could be they genuinely believe you are capable of much more and support you in your career. However, they could be trying to manipulate you. If you are perfectly happy in your current job yet your partner is pushing you to change, could it be they are trying to manipulate you into a position that pays better. Do they see your potential salary increase as making their life easier?

9) **Forced teaming**: in a healthy relationship, you will both have your own opinions, and you will also work well as a team. When one partner is manipulative, they will force you into a forced teaming situation. For instance, if your partner is having a disagreement with one of your friends about politics, they will also

speak for you as a unit. "We believe that the Democrats are ...." for example. Now, this is fine if you do have the same political beliefs, but if you have a different view, then they have robbed you of your opinion. When a partner uses this form of tactic, it can become routine and means that you lose your voice and individuality.

If you are constantly hearing the word "we" or phrases like "we are some team" or "we nailed that," and it makes you uncomfortable, then do something about it. Speak up and tell them firmly that you have your own opinions and points of view. If the behavior continues, then you need to halt the relationship and reclaim your independence.

10) **The silent treatment:** sometimes you can get so mad at someone you just can't find the words to say to them, so you say nothing. And that's fine, you are biding your time and waiting for your anger to subside. But if your partner is using this type of punishment regularly, they are manipulating you.

The Key Signs to Look for to Identify an Unhealthy Use of Silence

• When your partner is refusing to speak to you but is happily talking to other people in the same room. This indicates a sadistic side to their character as they are isolating you and making you feel less worthy.

• If your partner refuses to acknowledge you even when someone else refers to you. For instance, you are at a party, and someone asks your partner if you would like a drink. They then refuse to answer and act as if you don't exist. This is both humiliating and designed to make you feel ashamed.

11) **Using humor to shame you:** we all have our hang-ups, and your partner will know exactly what pushes your buttons. In a healthy relationship, they will be encouraging to you and help you to overcome your insecurities. If you have problems with your weight

or appearance, they will tell you when you look great and make sure you feel good about yourself.

Manipulators will take every opportunity to highlight your insecurities and use them to make you feel bad. Generally, they will couch their remarks in humor and make a joke out of your shortcomings. They are attempting to make you feel inadequate and worthless to maintain their dominance of you. If you feel confident or powerful, then you will find it easier to leave them.

12) They refuse to show emotions: when conflict occurs, a healthy partnership will have a discussion, air their grievances, and come to a resolution. Yes, there may be tears, raised voices, or anger. If your partner refuses to show you their emotions, they are trying to keep you in check. It isn't normal to be cool, calm, and collected all the time. Combine this with comments directed at you, suggesting you are the irrational one, and this is a form of gaslighting.

Remember that having emotions is normal. Try and encourage your partner to express themselves more when conflict occurs. If you can't elicit a response, then it could be time to seek therapy. There may be a deep-seated reason for your partner's lack of emotions.

Whatever the form of manipulation you may be experiencing, chances are you will be aware of the abuse on some level. If there is any hint of a warning bell ringing in your head, the least you can do is have a discussion. It doesn't have to be with your partner; you can try sounding out a trusted friend or family member. Somebody else may have a different perspective on what is happening and could help you to confront reality.

The worst thing you can do is to ignore what is happening and hope that it all gets better. Bad situations will only get worse, and you will get hurt.

Chapter 5: Psychological Warfare at Work

Consider how your normal day is split. Most people spend a third of their life in the workplace, especially on weekdays, so we would like to think it is a place where we can feel comfortable. However, because some people are competitive and, in some cases, spiteful, it can be an uncomfortable and stressful place to be.

If there are people who are displaying personality traits associated with the Dark Triad in your workplace, it can be detrimental to your health as well as your work. They will use unethical tactics to succeed and can be responsible for financial fraud and exploitation of the workplace.

Awareness is your key factor combined with vigilance in the workplace. Identifying colleagues with dark personality traits is not a clear indication of fraudulent practice, but it helps to put things in perspective. Some of the most successful leaders and professionals will display some of the traits indicated by the Dark Triad. For instance, focusing on achievements, self-confidence, and professional skepticism are all personality traits that can lead to career success. The key is to keep the negative aspects in check and avoid questionable behavior.

How to Detect Dark Personality Traits

Consider the following statements and how they apply to the people you work with:

Signs of Narcissism

- Boasting about their leadership skills.
- Routinely comparing themselves to established leaders.
- Constantly asking others for favors.
- Always at the center of attention.
- They only do work that has rewards and recompense.
- Brown nosing when in the company of VIP's.

Signs of Machiavellianism

- They are known for being sneaky and using any method to achieve results.
- They will use flattery inappropriately.
- Lack of empathy for co-workers.
- Regularly caught lying about irrelevant things.
- Can't be trusted to keep secrets and will use the information to belittle people.
- Will manipulate other people to achieve self-promotion.

Signs of Psychopathy

- Will take part in inappropriate behavior whenever possible.
- Has no remorse or morality.
- Will take risks without considering how their actions affect others.
- Has a turbulent lifestyle that appears to be spiraling out of control.

- They have a cruel streak.
- Lack of sensitivity.

We may all recognize at least one trait that could be applied to ourselves, and that is not a reason to panic. Some of the most successful people in present times and history will have a number of these traits. However, they will have a balanced personality overall and will know how to prevent them from becoming dominant.

If you are worried about someone you work with or have recognized any red flag behaviors, you have options. We will discuss these later once we have addressed other potential practices that could prove troubling.

Workplace Bullying

Studies have shown that up to 25% of people will witness some form of workplace bullying during their working lives. While we may feel we can identify people with dark personality traits, bullies can have a different set of behaviors. Some people believe workplace bullying is in your face and defined by individual actions. The truth is that it is normally an insidious way of controlling other people's emotions, psychological and physical behaviors.

Skilled bullies and manipulators can read people and exploit their weaknesses. They understand how to get under people's skin and use techniques to bully them into behaving in a way that suits the perpetrator.

Unfortunately, bullying often goes unnoticed in the workplace and can sometimes be accepted as a "normal" way of getting things done. The slow process of chipping away at an individual's emotional and psychological barriers will often be dismissed as it is difficult to spot and even harder to prove.

Luckily, it is emerging as a subject that needs addressing. No longer are people who are being bullied told to "man up" or "grow a pair" when they bring their grievances to light. Companies realize that this type of practice is growing and should be halted whenever possible.

Bullies are primarily looking to place their victims under duress to cause anxiety. This then leads to feelings of inadequacy, and they are more likely to bow to manipulations.

Classic Signs that Bullying is Occurring in the Workplace

Some bullies will use obvious tactics to intimidate other people and will use the following techniques:

• **Coercion:** verbal attacks can be used to make someone do things they don't want to. Using a loud tone or shouting will cause the victim to feel that they have no choice but to comply.

• **Humiliation:** using insults and embarrassing acts to belittle an employee or work colleague publicly.

• **Aggression:** someone getting up in another person's face can be a terrifying tactic to use in the workplace. It can make retaliation more difficult for the person being bullied, as it can be terrifying for the recipient and can cause excessive anxiety and stress.

• **Invasion of personal space:** if a co-worker is overly familiar or intrusive, it can swiftly lead to uncomfortable feelings. The bully will constantly invade your personal space, and they will feel entitled to tamper with your belongings. This type of bullying is designed to make the victim feel that they have no place to retreat to.

• **Offensive remarks:** we have all known some people who don't respect boundaries. This is a fact of life, but this type of behavior in the workplace can be more than offensive. When someone uses profanities, ribald jokes, or brings up unfounded rumors in public, they make the workplace an unsafe environment. People are entitled to enter their place of work without being subjected to bad language or unsuitable behavior.

- **Negative campaigning:** when a bully decides they want someone to leave their workplace, they can use an overt and underhanded campaign to persuade them to leave. This can be as subtle as a well-placed comment to colleagues about their victim not fitting in or being unfit for the position.

Or it can be as insidious as a full-blown email and online campaign to get the rest of the workforce to agree with them. Leaked emails and social media posts can be used to bully the employee into handing in their notice. The worst part of these campaigns can be the effect they have on the social interactions within the company. People are less likely to join a positive thread online than they are to join a negative campaign. Unfortunately, it is human nature to comment on negativity before positivity.

- **Underwork and overwork:** this type of bullying is quite common. It involves overloading someone with work one day and then starving them of tasks another day. This leads to a confusing state of mind when the employee is unsure if they feel overworked or underused. This will affect their work and lead to mistakes because they're unsure of their position.

- **Keeping a record of mistakes:** we all make them, and we all, hopefully, benefit from them. Mistakes are all part of the work process, but if someone is making notes about another person's worth, then they are bullying them. We are all capable of making our own journals or recording our shortcomings, but when you decide to do it for someone else, you are suggesting they can't recognize their own faults. This leads to feelings of self-doubt, and they begin to question their self-worth.

These subtle behaviors may be happening to you or to someone you work with. Maybe you recognize someone who uses these tactics? Whatever the situation, you need to be aware of the actions and the effects they have on others.

- **Deceit:** plain and simple lies. Do you know someone who is constantly being caught in a lie? Or maybe they are constantly being told lies without realizing it?

- **Diversion:** avoiding tricky subjects or situations when confronted with them. Changing the subject in discussions or canceling meetings and avoiding certain personnel.

- **Creating conflict:** is there someone in your workplace who enjoys pitting people against each other? You know the type; they cause a heated discussion and then walk away. This type of behavior is sneaky and destructive. When the conflict is examined later, they will have made sure their name is not connected to it.

- **Criticism:** we all recognize that constructive criticism is helpful, but unwarranted criticism is aimed at lowering morale. Do you know someone who is constantly putting people down without reason? Do they make inappropriate comments about appearance or personal subjects? This is insidious bullying and cannot be tolerated.

- **Taking credit for other people's work:** some bullies will take advantage of colleagues who may not be as experienced as them to steal their ideas. They will appear charming as they talk about projects and ask the other person what they think. Then they will use the ideas to gain favor and claim the credit.

- **Misinformation:** this is a common form of undermining someone. For instance, if an important meeting has been announced, the bully will "mistakenly" tell a colleague the wrong details. They may even hold back information that is meant to be passed on to make other people look incompetent.

- **Isolation and exclusion:** this is a devastating way of making someone feel uncomfortable in the workplace. We all want to feel part of a team, and being physically or socially excluded will make people doubt their self-worth. A common tactic would be to address members of a group individually while leaving out the intended victim.

• **Minimization**: this practice involves making light of someone's feelings. For instance, if the victim of bullying raises a point about something, the bully will belittle it. By persistently discounting someone's thoughts and ideas, the bully is making their victim shrink into the background and become a shadow.

• **Flattery**: some bullies will seduce their victims by complimenting them and using excessive flattery to make them appear trustworthy. They are offering a false sense of camaraderie and putting themselves in a position of power. If you believe that someone genuinely likes and admires you, then you are more likely to bend to their will.

• **Changing the goalposts**: some bullies in power will distribute titles and promotions at will. They replace different aspects of work without cause and change their responsibilities. This leads to a feeling of unknown and uncertainty. The victim then becomes more vulnerable and subject to manipulation.

• **They give backhanded compliments**: this is such a sneaky way of gaining the upper hand over a potential victim. The perpetrator will set their victim a task. If the task isn't completed, then they will berate them and make them feel ashamed. But if the task is completed, they will react in the following way. "Wow, I never thought you could have done that, well done you!" or "Who would have thought you were capable of that at your age? Great job." This makes them seem benevolent when, in fact, they are delivering stinging comments that will make the victim feel seriously confused. The bully has reinforced their position of having the upper hand while seemingly paying a compliment.

• **They refuse to validate other people**: workplaces should be a creative environment where ideas flow freely and receive the attention they deserve. Bullies will offhandedly dismiss other people's ideas with a cutting comment or a patronizing manner.

They will create the impression of benevolence but treat people like children who are incapable of adding value to the workplace.

What to Do if You Recognize that Bullying is Happening in Your Workplace

It is important to realize that attitudes are changing in the workplace. Bullying is no longer tolerated, and there are more litigious claims regarding bullying than there has ever been. With this in mind, most organizations realize that good workplace culture is a solution to costly, time-consuming legal battles.

Here Are Some Great Tips to Help You Prevent Bullying in the Workplace

1) Create a clear policy: there should be no gray areas about who is responsible for dealing with bullying. Human resources should have resources that deal with bullying behavior, and the consequences should be clear.

2) Train senior staff to recognize potential situations: the best place to deal with bullying is at a grassroots level. Once a situation has escalated, it may snowball until it becomes more serious. Having intuitive people in minor management will help to set alarm bells ringing earlier.

3) Promote an open-door policy: all employees need to know they have the right to air their views without fear of reprisals.

4) Speak to your employees: having healthy conversations about bullying and the potential harm it can cause is key. If you don't feel qualified, consider employing a professional speaker to address the staff and make them more knowledgeable.

5) Identify unacceptable behaviors: employees need to know that old fashioned subjects like racism, sexism, or any form of discriminatory speech will not be tolerated. Some people feel that if

these subjects are used in humor, it is acceptable. Make sure they know that times have changed, and so has the work-based culture.

6) Provide respectful feedback: no issue should go unresolved no matter how petty it may seem. Every employee should have a voice.

7) Document complaints: there should be written documentation of every complaint. This ensures that any recurring behavior is recognized immediately.

Chapter 6: Propaganda I: Political Propaganda

History has given us some amazing examples of propaganda, and two of the most striking forms originate from the Soviet Union and Nazi Germany. The two nations used effective methods of propaganda to influence their citizens into believing that their side of the story was the correct one.

They bombarded the population with varying forms of propaganda designed to persuade them to toe the party line.

Here Are Some of the Ways the Soviet Union Disseminated Propaganda

1) Schools and youth organizations: Stalin and his team of advisors recognized the best way to shape the future was to educate the youth of the present. They formed a program named the Young Pioneers for children aged between ten and fifteen years old, which taught their members to oppose the enemies of socialism. Children in Russia were surrounded by shrines to the Soviet leadership and were encouraged to learn songs and pledges that glorified the Stalin movement. Chilling images of schoolchildren wearing black uniforms while marching with banners were prevalent in the Stalin era.

2) Media: poor people in Russia had no way of accessing any form of entertainment, so the Russian propaganda machine used this fact to "educate" them and keep them informed. They installed radios into communal areas for poor people to listen to the news. They used the walls of subway stations to project propaganda films for those who could not afford the entrance fee to theaters.

3) Propaganda trains: Stalin soon realized that the use of the railway system was an effective way to reach his people. He authorized the use of propaganda trains filled with printing presses, projection equipment, radios, and public speakers to preach to the masses.

4) Posters: the use of posters as propaganda have been a common theme throughout different eras of Russian history. They regularly depicted the "new man," who believed that hard work and severe discipline were the best methods to overcome the more basic instincts of mankind. Images depicted the "common man" as a hero and created a division within the class system.

Common men and women were encouraged to view the bourgeoisie as an enemy. They promoted anti-religion and anti-American feelings, while vilifying the idea of "noble poverty."

5) The printed word: Russian people were only allowed to read newspapers that were favorable to the Communist cause. Any stories of crimes against humanity occurring on Russian soil remained unreported. Russian libraries were purged of "deviant" writers, and pre-publication censorship was introduced.

These methods were designed to encourage Russian people to band together and oppose any form of rebellion. People listened and watched the propaganda together and formed like-minded groups. Punishments for non-conformists were swift and harsh. It was impossible to tune out the noise of propaganda, as it was literally everywhere.

Propaganda in Nazi Germany

The emergence of Nazi Germany took political propaganda to a new level. Hitler was a master of propaganda, and he appointed Joseph Goebbels as the head of his campaign to convince the nation that the Nazi Party was seen in a positive light. He was also tasked to ensure the German people had no access to harmful information regarding the Nazi movement.

Goebbels collaborated with Albert Speer, a German architect and urban planner, to work with the SS and the Gestapo to launch a campaign of national "enlightenment." Their first task was to set up the Reich Chamber of Culture in 1933. This body of men dealt with all media sources of information like newspapers, film, and radio. To qualify for a position in the Reich Chamber of Culture, you had to be a member of the Nazi party.

Any disobedience within the organization was brought under control with severe punishments. Censorship was rife, and the Nazis controlled everything that the people read, heard, saw, and experienced. They understood that this was the optimum way to ensure that Hitler became the supreme leader of the German people.

When this happened in January 1933, the Nazi party was already in a position of strength. They felt strong enough to organize the infamous book-burning episodes that occurred just four short months after Hitlers' rise to power. Any book that didn't conform to the Nazi ideal was removed from libraries by loyal Nazi supporters. They were then publicly incinerated in huge piles, cheered on by Nazi followers. These public displays of power fueled the belief that the Nazis controlled the minds of the people.

The production of powerful propaganda films furthered this display of power. The films were made to highlight several issues and bring them to the nation's attention:

- The greatness of Hitler and his vision for the future.

- The Jewish people: the Nazis used beautiful and artistic posters to promote the hatred and fear of Jewish people and other non-conformist groups of people. They used beauty and art to mask the ugliness and hatred of the message they contained.

- The way forward for the future: they promoted the idea of a "master race" that began with "perfect children." Any imperfection was an insult to the Nazi vision of perfection.

- The mistreatment of Germans in Europe: as the approach of WWII became imminent, the Nazis recognized the need to demonize the rest of Europe. They did this by highlighting how badly migrant Germans were being treated in Eastern Europe.

The making of such films was not restricted to serious documentaries or news-based films. While films like *Triumph of the Will* (1935) addressed serious subjects, Goebbels also recognized the power of entertainment propaganda. He commissioned comedies and light entertainment films to give Germany a more human and lighter look.

Goebbels also recognized the power of saturation. He ordered the production of cheap radios so that every German citizen could own a radio. He also ordered loudspeakers to be set up in public, so everyone would hear the word of Hitler.

Before 1933 the Nazi party was the largest in Germany, but it did not have total support. Goebbels changed that fact and made sure Hitler took his place in history with a relentless campaign to win the hearts and minds of the majority of German people. He understood the premise of successful propaganda, and Goebbels is quoted as stating that once someone had succumbed to successful propaganda, they would find it impossible to escape.

Further into their campaign for world dominance, the Nazis recognized the use of other methods of propaganda. They used symbolism to its full extent. The use of the swastika, the salute, and uniforms made sure that people in the street recognized the power they held. While Hitler understood the importance of grandiose titles for his henchmen, he was astute about his own title. He refused to be called President, as he claimed the title was too "august" for him. This appealed to the common person, and Hitler garnered popular approval with this move.

Nazi Germany was a prime example of mass brainwashing. The Nazis used a barrage of information, images, and events to create an environment of hatred and reverence.

Political Propaganda in the US

As one election passes, the preparations for the next one begins. We are constantly being told to give our vote to one candidate or the other for different reasons. While this is a fact that nobody can escape, are we hardwired to believe the propaganda, or are we capable of making an informed vote?

Recognizing the techniques used is the first step to becoming a savvier voter. Let's examine some of the more popular ways that politicians have used propaganda while angling for our vote:

Presidential Ads

We need to travel back to 1952 to witness one of the earliest ad campaigns for a presidential candidate. "Ike for President" was a catch song used to promote Dwight Eisenhower. In 1960 JFK also used a catchy song to head his campaign. These were early examples of a popular method of propaganda called the "Bandwagon" technique.

The Bandwagon Technique

This is a technique that appeals to the masses and makes people feel part of a movement. This type of ad plays on the insecurities of the masses and the desire to belong. Take the example of a different type of ad. If you see a soft drink advert where masses of people are drinking the same product, it immediately makes you want to be part of the community. The presidential songs were catchy and inclusive and appealed to this type of voter.

The Testimonial Technique

Also referred to as the "endorsement" technique. The candidate uses various methods to boost their persona and appeal to a broader audience. These can include endorsements from political hard hitters, media outlets, sportsmen and women, and celebrities. They are believed to be persuasive cues for uninformed voters who have little interest in the candidates' policies or beliefs. They choose to select their preferred candidate by association.

While we are used to seeing politicians sharing the same platforms as famous people, a recent example was back in 2008 when Chuck Norris threw his support behind his preferred candidate. 2008 also witnessed the online-only advertisement by Barack Obama, which featured a host of famous people.

This type of technique can have a negative response. For every positive response, an association with fame can generate, there is the chance of a negative reaction. This is also referred to as a transfer technique. Highlighting the qualities of a well-known person works well with their followers, but they can generate feelings of dislike in the people who aren't so enamored.

Symbolism Technique

This is a method that appeals to a voter's heart. Remember that propaganda is a battle for hearts and minds, and symbolism is all about hearts. When a candidate is trying to appeal to a base feeling of patriotism, they will use all American symbols to stir the emotions. Think soaring eagles, Uncle Sam, good old apple pie, and flags. Lots and lots of flags. There is something about the American stars and stripes that appeals to the voter.

Nobody is suggesting that anyone looks at a picture of a flag next to a candidate and immediately thinks, "Hey, that flag makes me think you will make a great president," but it does talk to the subconscious. Throw in some glittering generalities, and you have an effective form of political propaganda.

Glittering Generalities

These are statements that use vague words and phrases to influence the public. They have no real meaning; they are mostly emotionally appealing and are designed to have a positive effect on the general population. They literally sparkle and make us believe in a better future and a positive outcome.

The words don't just sparkle; they leap out and give a sense of hope. Everything is going to be okay because this candidate says so! These types of statements have been referred to as "name-calling in reverse."

President Obama famously used the words hope, progress, and change to garner the support of America. We are all aware of the significance of the phrase "Make America Great Again" in 2016 and how that glittering generality appealed to certain voters.

The Plain Folk Technique

This is when politicians try to appeal to the man on the street. They may have had Ivy League educations and never known what it is like to "miss out," but politicians know how to appeal to the common person. George Bush and his son George W. Bush knew a thing or two about using the plain folk technique.

They knew that taking a scholastic approach to their speeches would alienate them from most of the population, so they made mistakes. These errors were designed to make them appear spontaneous and in touch with the average person. Telling the public that they are "a man of the people" can be a powerful tool, no matter what the truth.

Stacking the Cards

This type of propaganda may sound harmless, but it can be devastating. The perpetrator will highlight their personal accomplishments and triumphs without addressing any of their failures. They will then proceed to trash their opponent and drag their name through the mud. American politics is a hotbed of card stacking, and the ads used by candidates can be subtle, or they can use distressing images to suggest the opponent is at best useless and at worst evil.

If the images aren't enough, it could be time to use schoolyard tactics. Name-calling is a successful tactic for those not subtle enough to use other methods. Name-calling propaganda is used by governments and the media to describe groups that oppose their beliefs, who will be referred to as "terrorists" or "insurgents," while groups who support the government will be called "freedom fighters" or "activists."

It is little wonder that these tactics will then spill over into the political arena at election time. It has become the default epithet from both the "Left" and "Right" of politics. These tactics have been referred to as "Nazi-style" tactics. Some candidates bully their opponents by launching personal attacks, targeting individuals and giving them labels. We all remember "crooked Hillary," Dick Cheney being referred to as an "attack dog," Barack Obama being incorrectly labeled a "communist," John Kerry a "flip-flopper," and Joe Biden insulted with the nickname "sleepy Joe."

It really doesn't matter if there is any truth behind the accusation or not. The truth is that these sound bites make the new world of media hum. It thrives on the incessant profanity, trash talk, lies, and the general invective created by this type of propaganda.

Chapter 7: Propaganda II: The Manipulative Media

Consider how media-driven the modern world is. We watch news-media oriented programs on the television, the films we watch have hidden messages contained in them, and we are constantly subject to advertising. We communicate via social media, and every search we make online creates relevant advertising.

The term "media manipulation" is not one we use often, but we are all aware of some form of influence. Back in 2002, Sylvain Timsit, a well-respected French author, coined the phrase when he wrote about how political and economic powers use propaganda and other strategies to control the minds of the public. He became one of the first people to explicitly state the influence and control that mass media had on society.

The mass media is the largest form of remote control available. As people relax and prepare to be entertained, the manipulation of their thoughts and behaviors begins. They are presented with nuggets of facts and information that many people readily believe. They then use social media to share their thoughts and give them even more credibility. These "facts" will then be shared using the internet, cell phones, social media sites, and will travel the globe in minutes.

Consider why that information was presented to you in the first instance. Did it have verifiable sources, based on extensive studies and provable scientific facts, for example? Did it appear because the media feels the need to print and promote truths because it is in our best interests? Or do you feel that the information was some form of manipulation?

Some Strategies That the Mass Media Employs

Distraction

In 2014, Russia moved its military forces into the Crimea. There followed a series of events that would lead to alarm in the US and suggest a return to the Cold War era. The referendum held, the following annexation, and imposing of sanctions could cause a panic in the US, which certain agencies were eager to avoid. This story was superseded by the disappearance of Malaysian Airlines flight 370 and the mudslide in Washington State in the US. Classic distraction tactics used to keep the nation successfully focused on other matters. Acts of nature provide the media with certain elements of news. The number of deaths, potential miracles, and grieving relatives filled hours of news coverage.

Gradualism

This is a method that manipulates the public to accept socially unjust actions or events by conditioning them to the news gradually. For instance, if the government was going to close down certain institutions that would lead to layoffs, it would begin a gradual campaign against the institutions. This would consist of negative media stories about mismanagement, losses, drops in sales, and poor stock market figures. This prepares the public to accept the big news without tumult.

Scripting and Omissions

Most people think of *Time* magazine as a hard-hitting, truthful publication that can be trusted to give the people hard facts. It is highly regarded as one of the more relevant publications in the US and has a large readership. While these facts may be a version of the truth, in reality, some may perceive that *Time* magazine sanitizes its covers for US consumption.

It is standard for print magazines to have different covers to appeal to the target audience in different parts of the world.

Time magazine has a US cover, one cover to appeal to Europe and Africa, while the remaining two covers are aimed at Asia and the South Pacific. During the Obama years, *Time* chose to publish a cover depicting Vladimir Putin and his thoughts on the weak state of the US and the strength of the Russian union. Russia and the US have had a rivalry for years, so it is not surprising that he would call the US "weak" and Russia "strong." The heading was about Syria in Washington and defense in Damascus.

In fact, the gist of the headline was the only part of the cover to make the US version. While the other three covers showed the Russian leader, the US cover asked the question, "Is it time to pay college athletes?" and the headline became: "What Putin Wants," and "Syria: Inside the DC War."

Treating the Public like Children

Unbalanced news-reporting that seeks to rile up base instincts of fear, or dumb down serious issues, is a sure sign that some media organizations are determined to keep us under a blanket of ignorance. If biased media owners allowed us to see the cold hard facts, they run the risk of nurturing a generation of free-thinking individuals that are capable of critical thinking. They need us to be submissive, open to manipulation, and incapable of critical decisions that would challenge their power and wealth.

Manufactured Reality-TV

Reality TV shows are highly entertaining and cheap to produce, which is why there are so many on the airwaves. They draw the viewer in with the promise of real-life drama, tears, fights, more tears, and triumphs. They love to take a normal person and make them into a better version of themselves. This appeals to the viewers' psyche and tells them that they too can become a better person.

The truth is that these so-called reality shows are often scripted, or are carefully produced theatrical presentations. They rely on the viewers' gullibility and their ability to suspend belief to gain higher ratings.

Let's look at some of the common tricks that reality shows use to manipulate our beliefs:

• Frankenbiting: this is an industry term for editing clips and creating complete sentences from scratch. The producers will use different clips of conversation to create the content they require.

• The judges have no real power: in shows with a competitive element, there will normally be a clause that robs the judges of all power. As a viewer, we believe the judges are responsible for a particular contestant progressing, but the truth is different. At any point, the producers can step in and block the decision if they feel the decision will harm the show's ratings.

• Lying about schedules and budget: if you have ever watched a DIY show or you love *Extreme Makeover*, then you will know those amazing makeovers can be done in a short time with just a minimum budget. But can they? If a show is telling you that a bathroom renovation can be done in twelve hours for a couple of hundred bucks, chances are that it is a lie. They will have had a professional team working on the project for around ten days before the presenter steps in to film. Oh, and the budget is often completely unrealistic.

- Flawed people make better TV: reality shows know the power of portraying flawed people and exploiting their weaknesses. It allows the audience to feel superior and thankful for their lives and lifestyle. The producers will delve into the past of participants to discover what buttons to push. They will shamelessly use the contestant's personal experiences to trigger reactions. Unfortunately, because these people want to be on TV so badly, they will sign contracts that allow such intrusive behavior.

Digital Image Manipulation

During foreign or domestic conflicts, it is important to get a balanced view of the situation and decide for ourselves the merits of the decisions being made, right? The media have other ideas. They are using our basest emotions to influence our thoughts. Newspapers and news outlets around the world are at times guilty of manipulating images to influence public opinion. The ethics of digital manipulation is a gray area. You should be aware that sometimes the camera does lie.

Propaganda in Advertising

We have already discussed the role of propaganda in politics, so what techniques cross the stream with advertisers? Well, most of them! Think about it; politicians are trying to sell you the dream, the utopia they can supply if only you vote for them. Advertisers are doing the same. Your life will improve if you buy or subscribe to their product, so they use similar tactics as politicians.

Here are some ways they manipulate the public with advertising strategies:

Testimonial Propaganda

Just as politicians attach themselves to celebrities, so do advertisers. If Jennifer Aniston tells you that she uses a shampoo, then you immediately imagine yourself with shiny flowing locks just like her!

Another example was the Nike campaign to sell the world's best ball. Who do they have holding the ball in the advert? Wayne Rooney, a well-known soccer player who will represent the best and appeal to the customer.

This technique doesn't just involve celebrities. If you see someone in a white coat promoting toothpaste, you will immediately presume that they are a dentist. They have a professional air about them and a white beaming smile, of course you can trust them!

Bandwagon Propaganda

If you have ever been swayed by public opinion or peer pressure, you understand the bandwagon technique. You don't want to be left out, so you go with the majority. Advertisers realize this and take advantage of the fact.

A classic example is the golden arches of McDonald's. The red sign has the name of McDonald's with a statement underneath that reads "over ninety-nine billion served," which suggests a level of excellence. After all, if ninety-nine billion people have tasted their burgers, there must be something remarkable about them. So, who are you to argue?

Name-Calling

Just as the idea of politicians resorting to playground tactics should be ridiculous, so should this tactic in advertising. However, if a company stays within advertising rules, they can use this tactic without seeming harsh or mean.

If you have ever been in a situation where you are in direct competition with another individual, you will recognize the power of comparison. You may find that pointing out how you are better than your rival is a tactic that works. It may feel a bit mean, but it works so you can use it, right?

Similarly, in advertising, it is common to use a rival to highlight the different ways your product is better.

Once again, we turn to McDonald's for an example. However, in this example, they are the rival. Burger King showed an image of their Whopper burger sitting on top of a burger box. The slogan read, "Silly Whopper, that's a big mac box," conveying the message that the Burger King burger was too big to fit in the big mac box. Clever or sly? You decide!

Let's try another example. Select Harvest created a noodle product that was free from MSG. Now, they could have used that fact to promote their product and help people eat healthier, but they took another route. They pitted their product against a competitor that still had MSG listed as an ingredient. The tag line read, "How do you like your noodles? With or without MSG?" By posing the question, they are telling you that you, the customer, are responsible for deciding to eat healthily or for filling your diet with the harmful additive MSG. Powerful marketing with a moral twist.

Card Stacking

This type of propaganda has been used for generations and is one of the most common tactics in advertising. Highlighting the great qualities of a product while skirting any negative aspects make items more attractive.

How do they do this? Bold statements that shout about the superiority of a product are common. "This type of chip contains 30% less fat than regular chips." While that may be true, it doesn't make it a healthy option. However, the advertisement makes it look like some form of healthy foodstuff!

Cleaning products that claim to be 50% stronger than the original and have long-lasting qualities will fly off the shelves. Let's consider what the message is. Was the original product so bad that even a 50% increase in performance doesn't mean it will be brilliant? Who knows? These glib statements are meant to catch your eye and distract you from other products. If you buy the product, the job is done!

The truth is that propaganda is biased information and should be treated as such. Advertisers and the media are looking to control your thoughts and emotions to create the outcome they require. It's time to take our blinkers off and welcome a higher degree of truth into our lives.

Chapter 8: Mind Control and Brainwashing

When we think of mind control or brainwashing, it can seem like a concept straight from Hollywood. Images of mad professors with a hypnotic spinning spiral trying to make their patients fall under their spell. The attaching of helmets with electrical cables forcing the victim to become a drooling mind-dead zombie.

In reality, mind control techniques are commonplace in society, and we are subject to them every day. When mind control is used, the recipient may not know they are being manipulated as the techniques are subtle and sophisticated. Mind control is often a lengthy process that gradually changes a person's mind and makes them more susceptible to alternative ideas.

There is no physical force involved. Mind control is a relentless psychological process that applies social pressure on the victim to gain control of their thoughts. Everyone is susceptible to mind control, and that is what makes it one of the most dangerous forms of psychological warfare used today.

Brainwashing is a more aggressive process as the victim will be aware that they are being manipulated. They will understand that force is being applied to make them change their thoughts to align with the aggressor.

However, the early use of the word "brainwashing" was literal. In the early part of the 20th century, there were reports that the medical use of the term brainwashing actually meant washing the brain to cure certain illnesses. In 1934 *The Manhattan Mercury* reported a doctor recommending a patient should "begin with brainwashing. Every brain ... needs cleaning at some point."

In 1935 there was a medical exhibition based on the case of a young boy that had formerly suffered from the condition St. Vitus Dance. He was partially paralyzed, incapable of speech, and prone to fits. His brain was washed twice during four days of treatment, and the boy was cured.

With the dawn of the 1950s came a resurgence of the term. The meaning had changed somewhat, but the term resonated with people looking to describe totalitarian regimes. *The New York Times* reported cases of resistance fighters using the technique to transform weaker members of society into believers of their cause.

As the decade progressed, the term grew more popular. It became a popular way to describe consumers and gullible people who were being duped by advertisers to buy stuff they didn't need.

One of the earliest records of this use of the word is in *The Washington Post* in 1955. It describes how American children had been "brainwashed" into revering Davy Crockett, who was apparently a bad role model as he was basically a juvenile delinquent.

The use of the term brainwashing has now become more commonplace and is used to describe gentle persuasion by propaganda as well as the forced indoctrination meaning of the word.

Who Would Be Interested in Brainwashing?

Mental control is widely used to influence our thoughts and suggest certain ways of thinking, but is brainwashing still prevalent today? The simple answer is yes. We have already discussed the psychological warfare tactics we face every day, so realistically we are constantly being subjected to brainwashing techniques.

There is a fine line between mind control and brainwashing in modern society. Anything that attempts to bypass your thought processes and flip a switch that compels you to obey could be classed as brainwashing.

Manipulation Techniques

Chanting

There are parts of your brain dedicated to analytical thinking. One way to stop this process is to distract the mind with a repetitive phrase. The idea is to shut down any nagging thoughts that will make you doubt the message you are being bombarded with. During recent political conventions, the audience is encouraged to fill the gaps between speakers with repetitive chants. This stops the audience from having the chance to analyze exactly what the speaker has just said.

Planting the Seed

When you scan the internet for news or stories, you will be familiar with short, punchy headlines that tell you all you need to know. The people funding these stories have realized that very few people read the stories and are more likely to skim the headlines. They exploit this fact by planting keywords in the headlines that will manipulate your ideas.

For instance, if the opponents of a certain senator wish to denigrate his character, they can plant a headline that has come from an anonymous source.

Senator White: Cheating On His Wife For A Decade?

It is irrelevant that the statement is merely a question. The seed has been planted. Even if the following headlines appear, it will still have the same outcome.

Senator White Denies Affair

The Wife Of Senator White Confirms Rumors Of Affair Are False

If you are asked if you know who Senator White is, you will probably answer, "The guy who had an affair for ten years right?"

Repetition and Ridicule Fallacy

If you hear something enough times, you will believe it. No matter how ridiculous, if you are presented with "facts" in a certain way, you are hardwired to believe them. This is known as the appeal to ridicule fallacy.

Mocking an idea makes it less relevant. If you associate an idea, a person, or behavior with ridicule and shame, you will dismiss it. Alternatively, if a ridiculous idea is given gravitas and treated with reverence, it will seem more viable. Repetition is a powerful tool, and when teamed with a shaming technique, it can be effective.

Limiting Choices to Black and White Options

When we are put under stress, our brains revert to the fight or flight mode. This is a classic example of having only a black or white choice. When confronted with just two options, we will happily abandon our critical thinking circuitry and make a right or wrong move.

How many times have you seen arguments along the lines of?

"Do we fight the terrorists, or do we roll over and die like cowards?"

"Shall we all get loaded and go to a club, or are you a boring killjoy who doesn't know how to have fun?"

"You oppose the death penalty? So, you believe we should just let murderers roam free and kill again then?"

Using these types of "non-arguments" can trigger humans to shut down critical thinking—compelling them to "take the bait" so to speak, like trained dogs. It isn't subtle, but it appeals to the primitive part of the mind.

Mind Control in the Drug Industry

If you watched the movie *The Matrix* (1999), you might remember a scene when Neo had to choose between a blue and a red pill. The red pill represented his return to the real world, while the blue pill would send him back to sleep. Now, this is a classic case of using a simplistic metaphor to deliver a message to a cinematic audience, but it does have relevance in real life.

When you go to the pharmacy, you are subject to a form of mind control that is subtle but extremely effective. Pharmaceutical companies have used color to suggest an effect for decades.

Take the example of sleeping pills or aids to encourage better sleep. Look at the color of the pills and the packaging. Blue, blue, and bluer. Throw in a couple of fluffy white clouds, with a hint of blue, and the patient is already feeling drowsy.

In one study, patients were given the same sedative, but the color of the pill was changed. Half the patients took a blue colored version while the other half took an orange-colored version. The patients with the blue pills reported falling asleep 30 minutes sooner and sleeping an extra 30 minutes. This extension of a placebo effect suggests that if a patient is given the correct color of the drug, then the results will be improved.

Of course, governmental use of mind control is restricted by boundaries, and government agencies have never used sinister methods to control the minds of the nation. Or have they? Back in 1952, the US was undergoing a troubling period following the

Korean War. It was widely recognized that relations with the Soviet Union were strained, and the conflict had entered a new field of battle. The war had progressed to include the battle of the mind.

The CIA appointed Allen Dulles as director in 1953. He coined the phrase "brain warfare" and hinted at the need to expand the methods used to deal with the Soviet threat.

In 1953 the MK-Ultra Program was approved. This highly confidential program expanded the boundaries used to extract information from enemy agents and ensure they were unable to retaliate. They would use biological materials on their subjects as well as some chemical solutions. They approved the use of sexual forms of abuse and torture to gain results. Mind control methods such as isolation, extreme hypnosis, and deprivation methods were all considered suitable and effective.

The prime objective of the program was to develop a truth serum that would work effectively alongside other tried and trusted methods of extracting information. Proponents of the program attempted to use hypnosis combined with the effects of hallucinatory drugs like LSD to help their subjects recall even the most complicated details of physical objects or complicated information.

The use of LSD was perfect for the results they needed. Its chemical effects produced mental states that broke down the subject's character and left them unable to handle stress and anxiety. This allowed the operative to probe deeper without any resistance and gain the information they needed.

It has been reported that following the approval of the MK-Ultra program that over 150 human experiments were carried out using psychedelic drugs, paralytics, and electroshock therapy.

The objectives of the illicit program were clear. They intended to create substances that would:

- Heighten the subject's mental activity.

- Break down any barriers that would prevent them from disclosing information.

- Create a temporary or permanent state of amnesia.

- Enhance feelings of shock and confusion during interrogations.

- Produce temporary paralysis for shock value.

- Use isolation techniques to cause the recipient to become dependent on their captor.

- Lower self-esteem and create a feeling of worthlessness.

- Distort the subject's senses.

- Render them incapable of physical activity.

The other benefit of the program was to make American agents less susceptible to similar tactics if the enemy captured them.

As the program progressed, studies at some of the top universities in America conducted tests on LSD and deemed it too unpredictable for use in the program. MK-Ultra then sanctioned the use of ecstasy or MDMA, heroin, and other class A drugs.

Operation Midnight Climax

The project started in 1954 and involved a web of safe houses scattered around the country run by the CIA. It used prostitutes to lure clients back to the houses and dose them with a series of psychedelic drugs, including LSD. It is reported that the CIA allocated a whopping 6% of its overall budget to fund the program.

The program was conceived to use ordinary citizens to study the effects of these drugs, as recruitment of volunteers was drying up. This highly illegal program involved the prostitutes plying their clients with alcohol spiked with drugs and then having sex with them. Following the sex, CIA personnel would then observe the behavior of the men and use a two-way mirror to tape them for further studying in the future. Tapes of the men having sex with prostitutes ensured their silence. The shame of being found out prevented them from complaining about their treatment at the hands of agents.

Sometimes the sessions took a sinister turn. The experiments conducted on the subjects would often involve torture methods. Doctor Sidney Gottlieb was heading the program, and it is reported he took great pleasure in using sensory deprivation chambers and recording the results. He would then torture the subject further by replaying the most disturbing parts of the recording on a loop.

Some subjects were there consensually, and they were singled out for even more horrific fates than the unsuspecting subjects. Some volunteers were given mind-altering drugs for ten weeks or more without a break.

The MK-Ultra program carried on operating until well into the 1970s under different guises. In 1972 the tide was turning. It was rumored the lid was about to be blown off and the program exposed. The serving director of the CIA at the time ordered that all documentation attached to the program be destroyed.

In 1974 *The New York Times* wrote a damning exposé about the use of drugs and mind control techniques, which led to the formation of a commission to stop this type of experimentation.

The public was formally informed of the existence of such programs by the "Rockefeller Commission," carried out by then US Vice President Nelson Rockefeller. The commission highlighted the use of human subjects to create psychological weapons to use against enemies of the US. It was revealed that at least one fatality had occurred following illegal activities carried out by the program.

In modern times it can seem inconceivable that such methods were used on human subjects. However, times were different then, and it was thought the perceived threat warranted such programs.

Now we have much subtler methods of mind control, but who knows what happens behind closed doors? Especially closed laboratory doors!

Chapter 9: How Cults Work

The idea of the cult in the form we recognize is fairly modern. However, the use of the term has been recorded in England as early as the 17th century. The origin of the word is derived from the Latin term "cultus," which means culture or to cultivate. Modern Europe experienced a series of religious upheavals that saw the rise of a slew of new religions. Martin Luther split from the Catholic church and founded Lutheranism, a form of religion that spawned from the beliefs of the Catholic church.

The rise of Protestants in the 17th century led to major upheavals like the Spanish Inquisition. The term "cult" was used to describe the rebels who opposed the more traditional beliefs of Catholicism. The effects were not just religious; it spilled over into artistic and literary circles.

Use of the term then dried up for two centuries until the 19th century, when educated aristocrats and scholars began to take an interest in archaeology and long-lost religious practices.

Novelists soon recognized the appeal of such groups, and the word "cult" entered popular fiction. Any positive connotations soon disappeared, and the term became a byword for religious groups who were controlled by evil and practiced satanic rituals involving sacrifices and demonic worship.

Fast forward to the mid-20th century, and the term cult has become a derogatory way to describe any form of alternative religion or community that doesn't conform to regular beliefs. The alternative "hippie" lifestyle was ripe for embracing "cult" status. The use of drugs and the promotion of free love created a generation of young people who were ripe for exploitation.

Before we explore some of the more infamous cults, it is important to understand them. How they work, why they appeal to some people more than others, and some popular misconceptions.

The most common factor employed by cult leaders is mind control. Most experts agree with this fact and recognize that cults are led by people who are skilled at coercion and employ deceptive recruitment techniques.

Cults take different forms and are designed to appeal to all types of people. After all, a cult is only successful based on its membership.

1) Religious: possibly, the first type of cult experienced back in the 17th century. Religious cults use their belief systems to appeal to potential members and promise spiritual salvation.

2) Commercial based cults: these types of organizations appeal to the base emotion greed. They promise financial rewards if followers do what they are told. They will have a financially successful leader who epitomizes the wealthy future followers can expect. These cults use mind control techniques to persuade followers to work for free. They will produce motivational materials that followers will then pay for. The motivational videos, literature, and seminars will promise them success in the future but fail to mention that the cult leader makes his fortune from selling the motivational materials.

3) **Self-help groups**: we are constantly told that self-help groups, therapy, and improving our mental health are important. While this is true, some cults will use this fact to target vulnerable people. They may offer expensive courses to "improve your life," which involve being locked away at retreats and subjected to various group activities. They will use manipulative methods to create powerful emotional ties with the subject and validate the power of the cult. This leads to further courses and seminars that promise to advance the individual's improvement and, of course, cost even more. The only escape for many people from these types of cults is bankruptcy.

4) **Political**: the use of mind control and propaganda by Hitler and Stalin has already been covered earlier. These are classic examples of a cult mentality on a larger scale. Many of these methods have been seen again in recent times, from a number of current political leaders, in the way they seek to control elections and appeal to their "base" of followers.

Common Misconceptions About Cults

When we think about the term cult, it can conjure up certain images. For example, mass suicides of cult members.

These may have some basis in truth, but cults have infiltrated society by taking less obvious forms. If you want to understand the culture of cults, it is essential to recognize common misconceptions as well as truths.

All Cult Members Live in Communes

Cults thrive by using seclusion and isolation to control their members. In some cases, this means physically separating them from the outside world and forming self-sufficient communities. However, some cults are successful at creating a mental form of isolation. They encourage the "them versus us" mentality, which allows members to live and work in everyday neighborhoods and work in regular jobs. These people are emotionally and mentally isolated but present a functioning exterior to mask their fear or hate of outsiders.

All Cult Members Wear Robes, Chant, and Dress in Weird Clothes

Egotistical cult leaders may have guidelines for their members that dictate how they dress. More savvy sects and cults recognize the benefits of blending in. They encourage their congregants to hold down ordinary jobs and use their "normal appearance" to encourage others to show interest in their group.

Cults Are Led By Individuals

The ethos of cults is all about control. While their leaders define the most famous cults, it should not be an exclusive way of defining the term. Often a group led by a board of directors or a circle of "prophets" will use mind control to influence its members. Never dismiss an organization's motives based on its leadership methods.

Cults Encourage Large Families

The popular image of a cult is young girls, pregnant and barefoot with multiple partners and a horde of children surrounding them. Sometimes this will be true; the older generation will recognize the benefits of "homegrown" congregants who are less likely to leave the cult. They may allow multiple marriages and encourage free love.

Some cults operate with a different agenda. They limit or even ban their members from having children. They are more focused on encouraging their members to spend time recruiting new members or working for the group. The control that cults have over their members is what marks a cult, not the type of relationships or size of families.

Cults Are Small and Intimate

In the past, leaders of cults understood the power of personal interaction and influence. Most cults were limited to a certain number of people, hundreds of people normally but never more than a few thousand. Modern communication methods have changed all that. The internet allows cults to appeal to people worldwide, bridging cultural and language barriers with the use of translation apps and social media groups.

Some modern-day cults have used the internet to increase their membership proactively. Groups regularly appear on social media sites like Facebook and Instagram with enticing posts about their teachings and doctrines. The internet is every cult leader's dream; it allows that up close and personal contact they need with people who are thousands of miles away. Some cults have memberships that total hundreds of thousands or even millions, thanks to the internet.

Only Stupid People Join Cults

Having a doctrine that appeals to charitable people draws them in and gives them a sense of belonging. This is when the mind control and exploitation tactics are employed.

Intelligent and successful people often feel isolated because they are different. Joining a cult offers them a place to fit in, to be part of a bigger organization, and to do good. Another appealing aspect of cult life is the power to rise in the ranks. Many cults appoint people to a position of power that allows them to dominate other members, maybe financially or sexually. This appeals to their ego and overinflated sense of self-worth.

Should We Be Afraid of Cults?

When the term cult is used, it can be misleading. There is no meaningful distinction between most religions and cults. They encourage their members to commit to the ideals and beliefs of the group and preach the word to other people. Most religions ask for some form of financial commitment from their members, so why are cults different?

Psychological methods of distorting how their members act, think, and behave are the difference. Studying some of the more infamous cults will help us understand the distinction.

Extreme and Disturbing Cult Movements in Recent History

Sometimes it can seem like the US is the natural home of the cult movement with Charles Manson, L. Ron Hubbard, and David Koresh featuring heavily in historical accounts.

Here we explore some of the best-known cults alongside some of the lesser-known movements from around the world:

Aum Shinrikyo

In 1995 the world was horrified as the Tokyo subway was subjected to a Sarin gas attack. The perpetrators were found to be a Japanese religious group known as Aum Shinrikyo led by its charismatic leader Shoko Asahara. At the time of the attacks, cult membership was estimated to be around 10,000 in Japan and up to 45,000 worldwide.

The movement began as a yoga and meditation class in 1984 and appealed to quiet people who were looking for a spiritual way to practice yogic activities. As Asahara began to grow in popularity, he rebranded the movement and turned the group into a religious cult. He used bold statements, public interviews, and controversial ideas to recruit members. The group began to attract controversy in the following years, and it is reported that a cult member who tried to leave in 1989 was killed.

The group relocated to Western Australia and began to manufacture nerve agents and chemical weapons. It carried out attacks in various Japanese cities, which resulted in many fatalities. Police investigations failed to recognize the involvement of the cult and focused on innocent civilians. Following further atrocities, the involvement of Aum Shinrikyo was discovered, and twelve members of the cult were sentenced to death. Asahara and six other members were executed on the 6th of July 2018, with the remaining members executed twenty days later.

The Unification Church

In the 1940's the Unification Church, or as it is more commonly known, "Mooneyism," began life as a religious movement started by Sun Myung Moon. The group drew beliefs from various sources and recorded them in their "bible" Divine Principle. These were a mix of Christian beliefs, Asian traditions, and focused on the existence of a universal God. They preached the belief that all people deserved salvation, that Jesus was killed by mistake, and the second coming would be hailed by the birth of a male in Korea in the 20th century.

The movement moved its headquarters to the US in the 1950s. It continued to expand until it had reached 5,000 members in the late 1970s. Sun Myung Moon began to proclaim himself as the second coming during this period, and his movement received widespread criticism.

Arguments raged as the parents of young people used deprogrammers to remove their children from the cult. There was also a measure of support in theological circles for the Church, and experts urged a more measured consideration of the practices it carried out. As the Unification Church gained more acceptance in mainstream American culture, Moon was the subject of financial scrutiny by the government.

In 1982 he was convicted of falsifying tax returns and conspiring to defraud the US government. It has been reported that these charges were brought because Moon and his wife had pulled off a huge stunt in July of the same year. They "married" 2075 couples in a "mass wedding ceremony" in Madison Square Gardens while some American members replicated the ceremony in South Korea. Many of the couples were multi-racial and hand-picked by Moon.

In 1994 to mark the 40th anniversary of the founding of the Unification Church, it was announced a new organization would emerge. The Family Federation for World Peace and Unification became a significant force in the religious community and encouraged sexual morality and interracial reconciliation.

The term "Moonies" has become a derogatory term for anyone expressing a desire to join a cult-like movement.

Jonestown

Jim Jones founded the cult movement known as the Peoples Temple. He is infamous because, in 1978, he engineered the biggest mass murder-suicide in American history. Jonestown was a utopian community in the depths of the jungle in South America. On the 18th of November, Jones had led a murderous attack on a U.S congressman and three members of the media in Guyana's capital city Georgetown. Later in the day, he laced a batch of fruit punch with cyanide and urged the members of the group to drink it.

The majority of people complied, although some cult members were thought to have been injected or shot. The expression "drinking the Kool-Aid" relates to what is known as the Jonestown massacre, and it epitomizes the bandwagon form of propaganda and psychological warfare. Over 900 Americans died that fateful day, proving the power of persuasion and mind control can prove deadly.

The Manson Family

Arguably the most famous cult in history was led by Charles Manson, who established a home for his "family" in the San Fernando desert of California in the late 1960s. He encouraged the use of hallucinogenic drugs and the summer of love ethos. Manson proclaimed himself a messiah and encouraged his followers to worship him and follow his every whim. In November 1968, Manson met a showbiz manager who mentioned he was renting his house to showbiz royalty Roman Polanski and his wife, Sharon

Tate. Manson formed a plan to send his most trusted devotees on a murderous mission to kill the pair. He planned to spark a race war that would lead to a global apocalypse, allowing him to rise to power.

The Manson Family devotees murdered several victims in 1969, but the most shocking occurred on August 9th. Manson told his followers to murder the pregnant actress Sharon Tate and kill anyone else who was at the property. The four other people at home were murdered alongside the eight-month pregnant actress in a bloodbath that shocked the police officers that attended the crime scene.

The following evening Manson accompanied other members of his family to carry out a further double murder. They tied up and tortured Leno and Rosemary LaBianca at their home in the Los Feliz area of Los Angeles.

The two-day murder spree has become one of the most infamous examples of how dangerous cults really are. So, should we be afraid of cults? We should be informed, aware of the power of cults and sometimes fearful. It doesn't pay to ignore the real and pertinent danger that cults represent.

Chapter 10: NLP and Dark Negotiation Techniques

What is NLP?

The term NLP represents Neuro-Linguistic Programming. In the 1970s, Richard Bandler and John Grinder developed NLP, after studying successful people in the field of communication and negotiation. They discovered the common methods used to persuade and manipulate other people to bend to their will.

This resulted in a program of techniques that concentrate on how the body, the mind, and language work together to provoke certain changes in a person's behavior and make them better negotiators. They discovered how different people grasp the power of language, while others are conscious of more physical behaviors.

NLP works because most people base their reactions on the information available. NLP, as a positive force, assumes that everyone can use the program to achieve their own physical and spiritual goals. It has also been discovered that these same techniques can be used for darker purposes to manipulate other people into doing things they are less than willing to do.

The truth is that NLP can be used with good or bad intentions. If someone is uncertain about progressing with their ambitions or desires, NLP techniques can be used to nudge them forward. If you feel that someone's decision-making process is taking a turn that could be harmful, then the same techniques could alter their decisions. These are good intentions, right? But they can also be used to make people do things that aren't as honorable.

Are You Being Subjected to NLP Techniques?

If you feel that certain people have an unhealthy influence on you and fear they may be manipulating you, it can be uncomfortable. Do you find it impossible to say no to certain people? Are you being manipulated?

Signs That NLP is Being Used

1) **They may mirror your actions**: pay attention to the people around you. Are they mimicking your body language? When you cross your legs, are they doing the same? Try brushing a strand of hair away from your face and seeing if they do the same movement immediately after. Mirroring is a natural and often instinctive behavior between people who are comfortable with each other, but some people consciously use this as a powerful NLP technique to encourage trust. Some people are more adept at this than others, but if you pay attention, you should notice if the actions seem contrived and insincere.

2) **They may use twenty words when one would do**: do you have people in your life who use vague, wishy-washy language to say a lot without actually saying anything? For instance, a sentence like "I see you are aware of your personal space and the relevance it has on your physical being, but you are unaware of the barriers you erect to fulfill your self-discipline, while allowing others to float above these

barriers and observe you." NLPers love this sort of language, which makes them seem knowledgeable and spiritual at the same time.

3) **They insist on rapid decision making:** do you have work colleagues who are constantly asking you to make snap decisions? Maybe a boss who pressures you to say yes or no at a moment's notice. Most people need to think things over and take their time making decisions. People using NLP recognize it is easier to manipulate people when you put them under pressure. They will use layered language to influence you like, "We need to make brave decisions quickly; if we don't, we will look incompetent and unprofessional." This type of language is designed to make you feel a lesser person if you don't comply with the initial pressure.

4) **They will give you permission to do what *they* want:** this can be a tricky technique to spot. If someone is using it to produce negative results, they will use permission pressure to influence you. For instance, if they want you to give them something, they will pressure you with language: "Go ahead and begin your new selfless life, start with me! Feel free to let go of your selfish nature and share your fortunes with me!"

The idea of these techniques is to make you feel like you are in charge of your own decisions and the paths you choose. They sound twisty and deceitful when you analyze them. Be wary of these techniques and resist being taken advantage of.

Dark Negotiation Techniques

We all must negotiate. It could be as simple as getting your kids to go to bed or as complex as negotiating a new contract at work. Negotiations will play a major part in all our lives. If you know someone who always seems to come out on top when negotiating, the chances are that they know the following tactics and use them to gain the upper hand.

Become Better at Negotiating

Try these negotiation hacks to help you get what you want:

1) Always look disappointed: successful negotiators are aware of the power of disappointment. Even when they are secretly overjoyed with an offer, they know that feigning disappointment will benefit them in the following ways:

   • They will be able to ask for more because they seem unhappy with the current proposed deal.

   • If they show happiness at the current offer, you may feel you have overstated the deal's worth. This may lead to you reducing or reconsidering the offer.

2) Answer with questions: whenever possible, keep the interaction flowing by using questions to answer queries. For instance, your negotiator may state, "You need to do better than that." You then reply with, "Just how much better?"

3) Point out that defensiveness is not a great quality: if a situation is getting heated, you need to release tension with a laugh. Powerful negotiators recognize the power of humor and will use it to put their opponents on the back foot.

4) Invent a higher authority that dictates what you can do: if you have ever negotiated a price for a car, you will most likely have encountered this technique. Real power negotiators will paint themselves as a low-level operative when it comes to the final say. This means they can halt discussions because they need to consult with a higher authority. You are then left to mull over your offer and reconsider your position. When they return, they can then adopt the good cop, bad cop stance and tell you they did everything they could, but the guys upstairs won't budge.

How to Deal with These Tactics

- Pretend to believe them but make a mental note of the tactic.

- Call the person out on the good cop, bad cop thing.

- Feign interest in meeting the "guys upstairs."

1) Last-minute changes in a deal: creating a last-minute dilemma is a classic manipulation tactic. When a deal isn't struck yet, the other person can claim that a higher authority (possibly referred to as "the board") is interfering with it.

Try this type of blindside in response: "Okay, I hear what you're saying. The trouble is I really want to keep to my side of the deal, but as you were dealing with the board, I had time to crunch some numbers, and the truth is the market has changed. There is more demand for my product, and as such, I will need to charge you a 10% surcharge. I realize this is short notice, so I am willing to drop this to 5%, but I need to know by the end of business today."

2) Use the power of location: you may not realize, but when you are negotiating, whoever is on the home ground has a distinct advantage. If you begin your negotiations by agreeing to meet at their office or their chosen location, you have given the first concession. Try and avoid this by having a say in the meeting venue. A neutral spot will give you an equal playing field.

3) Bringing backup: If you ever feel outnumbered in negotiations, it can mean the opposition is playing negotiation games. If they circle you or all sit opposite you, they are trying to create an antagonistic frame of "us versus you," which is designed to intimidate you.

Try this Powerful Move to Put You in Charge

If more than one person shows up to discuss the deal, try saying this: "Hey [insert name], it is so nice to see you. I was expecting a more personal approach today. The more people that get involved, the more likely it is to get complicated. I can recommend a great coffee shop where these guys can grab a quick drink. It won't take long for us to get this sorted."

Not only have you dismissed the extra people who have shown up, you have taken the upper hand in negotiations and have also suggested that it will be a rapid meeting, and you already know the outcome.

1) The nibbling technique: also known as squeezing the last drop. The more manipulative a negotiator is, the more they will try to get from a deal. Just as you are reaching for the pen to sign the deal, they will drop a bombshell asking for just a little bit extra.

2) Pretend to notice a defect: this is another last-minute tactic designed to elicit extra concessions from you before you sign. They will point out something they claim to have failed to notice and ask for a discount. Stay strong and tell them the price is fixed or try this other negotiation-busting technique. Tell them if they drop the delay tactics, then lunch is on you. Then feel free to walk away immediately after the deal has been sealed.

10) Use online resources to level the playing field: if you are in a position of power when closing a deal, your opponent may stick to electronic mediums to negotiate the outcome. Don't panic, they are trying to get one over on you, but you are aware of their game. Suggest that a face to face meeting should occur, but you can discuss the details online. This helps you gauge their reasons for avoiding personal meetings.

Other NLP Methods

NLP is not just about manipulating other people. It is intended to be a manual for your brain that can transform your life completely.

Try these NLP techniques to manifest a better future for yourself:

1) Dissociation: what are the worst-case scenarios you face regularly? Do you panic when faced with public speaking, or get shy in the presence of members of the opposite sex? Try the following steps to help alleviate these crippling emotions:

- Identify when you are feeling uncomfortable and not fully in charge of your emotions.

- Imagine yourself rising above your physical body and looking down on the situation. You are simply an observer, and your feelings will change as you continue to watch.

- Float back to your physical self and bring the feeling of calm you are experiencing with you. If you feel panic occurring, repeat the process until you feel comfortable.

2) Content reframing: this technique is all about getting things in perspective. For instance, maybe you have lost your job. You may be distressed at first, but you need to change your experience. You are now free to try a different career. You could decide to start your own business, instead of becoming fearful and panicking, focus instead on the positives.

3) Create rapport: you can try to create empathy and connection with another person by mirroring their body language during a discussion. Mirroring will often occur subconsciously between two people who share similar interests or a close bond. Of course, mirroring is just part of the package and won't make people like you if you are a horrible person. It is just a gentle nudge to pay attention and get others to share a rapport with you. If they smile, you smile. If they tilt their head when talking, then you might do the same. Try verbal mirroring and lower your voice when they do. If you pick up certain terms they love to use, then incorporate them into your conversation.

In short, NLP techniques can be used to make yourself a better person. This will help you gain friends and become more confident.

You will project an improved version of yourself that others will naturally gravitate towards.

It cannot be stressed enough; the NLP methods can be both positive and negative. How you use these techniques is a personal choice. Be aware that using psychological warfare is a significant way to change people's lives. Use them carefully.

Chapter 11: Cybercriminals

It is important to define the term cybercrime to understand how cybercriminals operate. In 1981 Ian Murphy, who was also known as Captain Zap, became the first person ever to be convicted of computer-related crime. He hacked into AT&T's computers and changed their internal clocks. This allowed customers access to late-night discounts during daylight hours.

Three years later, in 1984, the Secret Service received jurisdiction over computer-based fraud, which led to Congress passing an act that stated hacking into computer systems was considered a criminal act. The first large scale attack was in 1988, when $70 million was stolen from the First Bank of Chicago. This led to a slew of attacks as hackers became more prevalent and successful. Stories of teenage hackers infiltrating government websites appeared in the media, and "hacktivist" groups began to form.

In 2008 the Pentagon officially declared cyberspace the "fifth domain of warfare," which identified the growing threat posed by cybercriminals.

What is Cybercrime?

It is the use of cyber networks to gain illegal access to data and information held by other people. This can include national websites, Governments, corporations, retail online organizations, banks, and individuals. When we use our personal computers, we should be able to feel safe. We should be able to trust that our information is not at risk from fraudulent sources and cybercriminals. This, of course, is seldom the case.

Cybercriminals target anything and everyone. They are interested in anything that can be used to create profit. This could involve trading military or trade secrets, or as simple as the theft of credit card details or PINs for debit cards.

New technologies inevitably create new criminal opportunities, but that doesn't necessarily create new forms of crime. Cybercrime is an online form of theft for traditional criminals who can use a computer. Fraud, child pornography, and identity theft all existed before the emergence of the computer, yet they have all been linked with the umbrella term of cyber-crime.

The important distinction to understand is that cybercrime has a nonlocal character. It has opened worldwide opportunities for those who seek to benefit from criminal activities. The planet-spanning benefit of the internet offers such a vast array of opportunities for criminals; it has created some gray areas of legality. For instance, if a person who lives in a country with strict laws against certain types of pornography then accesses such material in a country that has less stringent laws, are they subject to that country's laws or the ones of their resident country?

Where does cybercrime take place? There are methods for cybercriminals to hide their tracks and disguise their online presence. However, just as traditional police forces can track physical criminals, some cyber professionals are trained to uncover a cybercriminal's tracks.

Common Forms of Cybercrime

Quite simply asking what types of crime are carried out online is like asking a law student to list every type of crime committed in the world. While we are aware of cybercriminals hacking into major organizations and causing worldwide disruption, this often does not affect our daily lives. The crimes most pertinent to individuals often involve some sort of fraud or theft.

Cybercrimes That May Affect You

The Nigerian or the 419 Scams

Before the advent of online crime, this scam was used with both traditional snail mail and later with faxes. The scam involves a request from a "Nigerian prince" who has millions of dollars tied up in an account in Nigeria and needs a bank account to transfer it to. The recipient will be asked for a small upfront fee to help move the money out of the country with the promise of receiving a larger sum in the future. Of course, the money never materializes, and the scammer will often ask for further money, and some victims have been scammed out of hundreds of thousands of dollars.

ATM Fraud

Cybercriminals love a mundane yet simple way to make cash. They have developed a way to record data from customers' cards at the ATM and then they hack the bank records to gain access to PINs. They then create imitation cards to withdraw large amounts of cash illegally. The problem is on the increase, as ATMs are the preferred method of withdrawing cash across the globe. ATM theft has become a growing international problem.

Wire Fraud

We quite happily transfer funds online to pay bills and purchase online items. Nobody seems to carry cash anymore, and this is manna from heaven for cybercriminals. There are examples of cybercriminals who gain access to a bank's database and transfer just

$1 from each account. These types of transfers fly under the radar and can remain undetected for months. Huge sums have been stolen using wire transfers.

Piracy

While most of us will have been offered counterfeit DVDs and compact discs, we all know that it is illegal. Most people will recognize the crime as theft, while others will consider it their given right to take advantage of this offer of free entertainment. But what if our jobs were hijacked in the same way? What if people expected the goods and services that we supply to be free? That would be a crime, right? So why don't we pay the same respect to the jobs of people in the entertainment industry? Piracy is a crime.

Identity Theft

Most of us remember the episode of *Friends* (1994) when a fun-loving lady stole Monica Geller's identity with hilarious results. The actual crime of identity theft is possibly one of the most insidious ways that cybercriminals can affect your life. The only piece of information a criminal needs in the US is someone's social security number, and they can then steal their identity. They have access to all the documents related to that person's citizenship. They now have the power to set up a completely separate identity using the victim's name. They can acquire a driving license, open bank accounts, and run up loans. They operate on many different levels. The smallest amounts may be as low as $300, while some amounts are higher. Most Americans are aware of the possibility of identity theft and are more vigilant, which means the amounts have dropped in recent times.

Spam

If you have an email address, then you will have been sent spam of some sort. This is unsolicited emails containing advertisements or links to sites that can be at best, useless, and at worst, offensive. Spam may seem like a normal part of cyber life, but it is a crime.

Worse still, it is a crime against all users of the internet. It is impossible to see how spam can be eliminated without violating the freedom of speech we all enjoy. Most of us are protected by the email providers we use, but we could all benefit from extra measures of security.

These types of crimes listed are just scratching the surface of those committed by cybercriminals. We need to know how to protect ourselves online just as much as we protect ourselves in normal life.

Protect Yourself Against Cybercriminals

The internet is not a benign place that is safe for all users. While we expect some form of protection from the social media and sites we use, we can also put some additional precautions in place. These are not just suitable for tech-savvy users but can be used by every single person who knows how to turn a computer on!

1) Use strong passwords: do you have the same password for every site you use? Is it a combination of your birthdate and a pet's name so you can remember it easier? Did you know that around 70% of adults use the same password for multiple sites? You need to change that fact! Make your passwords complex. Change them regularly. Make use of symbols, numbers, and at least ten letters that are not necessarily sequential. Use a password management app to keep a record of your new, complex passwords, and don't rely on your memory.

2) Make sure your software is updated regularly: cybercriminals are always searching for flaws in software packages. They then have a limited period of time to exploit these flaws. If you are regularly checking the package you use, you can remain one step in front of them.

3) Use a VPN: a VPN or virtual private network is a must for anyone spending time online. It protects your online privacy and

makes it more difficult for hackers to trace you and your activities. You can choose a low-cost VPN from various providers to make your location and information anonymous. VPN's encrypt all the data you send and keep you safe. VPN's are legal in most countries apart from China and Iraq, but there can be anti-privacy and censorship requirements, so make sure you check the information for your region using vpnmentor.com.

4) Back up your files regularly: use a separate storage system to store your files so you can clear them from your computer. Just like a clean house protects your physical health, a clean computer prevents online viruses and corruption.

5) Be careful what you click on: cybercriminals are waiting to lure you in with a catchy advertisement or an appealing link to a site. Never download a file from an unknown source or click on a link that isn't generated by a legitimate source.

6) Keep your financial details private: how many times have you read about bogus emails or other communications from banks asking for account details? Cybercriminals understand a legitimate-looking email will make some of us disclose our security details. Talk to your bank, and you will soon discover that they will never ask you for any details or request that you transfer money into alternate accounts.

7) Manage your social media settings: most people have at least one social media account, while many people have multiple accounts. Imagine removing the hassle of managing these accounts with just one online tool. Try CoSchedule.com for advice on how to manage your personal and business media accounts. Take Twitter, Facebook, Instagram, and Pinterest accounts and make them more secure. This type of security will help you to protect your online life and the details you reveal.

8) Understand identity theft can happen anywhere: when you leave the security of your own home, you are often putting yourself at risk from cybercriminals. When you are traveling, you may need

to get information on the road. This can enable hackers to gain an insight into where you are, what hotel or resort you will be visiting, and how you are going to pay for them.

How many times have you seen friends or family using social media to advertise the fact they're going on holiday? It is normal to get excited about holidays and traveling, but declaring you are about to be away from home for two weeks is an invitation to regular thieves as well as cybercriminals. Take your VPN with you and keep the details of your trip quiet until you return home.

9) Talk to your kids about the dangers of the internet: because your kids have a clean slate regarding credit histories, they can become a target for criminals who specialize in identity theft. Explain to your children what they can and can't share on the internet. Make sure you have access to their social media accounts, and you can manage their security settings.

This is also the perfect time to tell them about the dangers that can lurk online. Nobody wants to scare their kids, but telling them to be vigilant is imperative. They need to know they can come to you if they fear they are being groomed or are facing harassment online. Bullying has reached new heights with the internet, and your kids could be at risk of online bullying and stalking.

10) Be aware of what to do if you are targeted: remember that nobody is safe online, and if you notice any abnormalities on your computer, you should report it. Inform your local police force, and they will help you decide what to do next. There are plenty of resources out there to keep you safe. If you think your financial details have been accessed, cancel all your cards immediately and get in touch with your bank.

Cybercrime is not restricted to spy novels and thrillers anymore. Online crime is fast becoming the number one way that criminals operate. The predicted cybercrime damages for 2021 is around $6 trillion just for the US. Don't become part of this statistic. Use the tips above to keep your online experience enjoyable.

Chapter 12: Protecting Yourself

Have you ever wondered why you feel strongly about some subjects, yet others pass you by? Are your opinions fueled by outside influences, or are they a true reflection of your beliefs?

We live in a democratic society, so surely, we are encouraged to think freely and form our own opinions? You would think so. But the truth is that democracy, in its purest form, is all about manipulation. We need to be told how to think and what appeals to us by people who we will never meet. If we weren't educated to think that way, our society would be in chaos.

The trouble with modern society is it seems to have taken this concept a step too far. We are subject to thinly veiled propaganda that presents itself as news. We are presented with the "facts" and information that people in powerful positions feel we should see. Misinformation and propaganda are easily spread via social media and biased online "news" websites. If it's a biased niche "news" website, whether on the left or right of the political spectrum, or a tabloid, then it is important to independently verify any "facts" and to filter out the opinions and agenda of the media organization in question. In short, we are often being treated like children, and if you look closer, you'll see when there are blatant attempts to appeal to our emotions and biases, instead of clearly presenting facts in an impartial manner.

In a nutshell, we need to stop accepting dumbed-down versions of reality and take an active part in what we absorb. Short buzz feed style headlines that grab the attention and keep us flicking from subject to subject tell us extraordinarily little, yet plant seeds of misinformation in our psyche.

Here are some ways to make sure the information you receive is relevant:

Choose Your News Source Carefully

Some news sources are more reliable than others, and some journalists are more ethical than others. This doesn't mean you can accept people's opinions or statements as facts—such as those often made in short captions on Twitter or social media—without independent verification and evidence that they are true. A lot of "false news" is spread in memes, tabloids, or on niche and highly biased "news" websites, and via social media. It is important to find reliable sources and to investigate further, using critical thinking, before believing such information. You should be presented with a balanced argument that contains any possible biases and which comes from a reliable and ethical source—not from an opinion piece, a biased headline, or statements on social media that promote conspiracy theories or can easily be proven as outright lies.

Once you start questioning the facts you are presented with; you will learn to separate propaganda from reality. There are so many sources providing you with "news" that it can feel overwhelming.

Reliable Sources That Produce Quality Journalism

1) *The Wall Street Journal:* when you choose to read the WSJ, you know what to expect. The publication produces highly accurate

articles with a conservative bias. Once you accept this, you can rely on it to supply you with information that has come from a trusted source.

2) *The BBC*: this well-known British institution is respected across the globe for its accurate content and lack of bias. When the BBC reports on political stories, it focuses on what politicians have said and little else. It doesn't use its own views to influence viewers, which is something that can't be said about most US news networks. The BBC's commentary is generally factual and trustworthy.

3) *The Economist*: this publication has been around for over 150 years and has a liberal stance about most stories. It is a trustworthy source of news with clear facts. *The Economist* publishes opinion pieces as well as straightforward news stories. However, it clearly states that opinion pieces are exactly that, the journalist is stating their personal opinion and trying to persuade us to agree. *The Economist* is a serious source of intelligent and trustworthy news and is considered the most trusted news source in the US.

Read More

While the news is important, it should be balanced out with other reading matter. Try nonfiction books to widen your understanding of the world and enjoy a classic piece of fiction instead of turning on the television. Read widely about history, theology, or scientific subjects. The mind is capable of great things if only you give it some information to work with.

Don't Take Sides in Politics

You can only get a balanced view of a subject by considering all sides. You will have a bias; we all do, but if you only listen to people who have the same views as you, how will you form a balanced opinion? Try being a devil's advocate and read literature as if you were a supporter of the opposing party. If you can cast your affiliations to one side, you will become a more informed voter who can take part in political debates with confidence.

Become a Clear Thinker

Now you have reliable sources for your news; it's time to address how you think about other aspects of your life. Are you swept up by popular opinions and find yourself agreeing with statements just to fit in? That is not healthy, you are an individual, and it's time you asserted yourself as the free-thinking version of yourself.

Ways to Clear Your Mind and Think for Yourself

Create a Healthy Mind Space

Have you always got your mind on your social media, or do you constantly check emails and your phone for messages? Remember the good old days when we didn't feel the need to connect to everyone 24/7? Maybe you don't; maybe you are too young to remember those bygone days when we could just turn off for an hour and give our brains a rest. If that is the case, it may be more difficult for you to imagine an hour a day without stimuli from your electronic devices.

However, giving your brain a chance to breathe will be an eye-opener for everyone. We are bombarded with requests, nuggets of information, or we feel compelled to fill every minute with tasks. What happened to alone time? Why do we feel that time spent alone isn't relevant?

Call it meditation, call it recouping your mental ground, call it "me time." Whatever you call it, just do it. That means no phone, no laptop, no television, no book, and even no radio or music. You are about to meet your brain and have a meaningful chat. Enjoy!

Refuse to Be Pushed into Anything

We are surrounded by click-bait forms of media and information. It requires instant decisions, and uninformed replies. You may be used to seeing a post online and replying in seconds.

This is a form of addiction and must be stopped. The world will not implode if you fail to comment on what your friend thinks about a cute puppy post.

Ask questions about what you see. Is it relevant to your life, and will you benefit from any aspect of it? If the answer is no, then ignore it. Don't be a sheep, don't follow popular opinion just to fit in. Be the person who questions the preconceived notions we are all subject to.

Give Yourself Time to Consider All Options

If you need more time to consider your decisions, then say so. Be firm and tell the world you are not going to be pushed around. It may seem like an alien concept the first couple of times you try it, but as your confidence grows, so will your resolve.

Learn from Mistakes

We all make them; we all see others make them. Mistakes, errors, flaws, and gaffes are all part of human life. Why then are we made to feel like a failure whenever we make them? Hold your hands up, admit you were wrong, and encourage yourself to learn from mistakes. Other people will see you are willing to admit when you are wrong and respect you for it.

How to Avoid Being Manipulated in Relationships

We have discussed how psychological warfare can affect relationships and lead to one partner being the manipulator. If you feel the situation is completely out of control, then you must end it. But if there is a chance to make something happen to improve the relationship, then you should try.

1) Ask your partner something fresh and exciting: if you have been together for some time, it could be that communication has become a habit. "How was your day?" and "What happened at

work?" are boring when asked daily. Try making an effort and asking something you really want to know. Try questions like: "What was the best memory of your childhood?" or "Have you ever dreamed of traveling in space, and what do you think it would be like?" When you put in extra effort to create a meaningful conversation, you show your partner another side to you. You want to know more about them because you love them.

2) Make time for them: both of you should be able to have independent activities, and this is important. However, sometimes we can be inflexible when tweaking our schedules in case it seems like we are showing weakness. Try compromising. Maybe you could drop that spin class or gym session to go to that movie premiere they want to attend. You shouldn't have to make sacrifices, but compromises are fine.

3) Let go of the past: if you have had concerns about past behavior, then you need to draw a line under it and move on. By agreeing to try again, you are saying you forgive them. This means you can't let past issues affect your future.

4) Remember the small things: sometimes, we worry too much about grand gestures and overblown displays of affection. Small details can be just as important. For instance, if your partner mentions they need to have an important meeting with a client next week, then make a note of the day they are meeting. When your partner arrives home that evening bring up the subject. They will be pleased you remembered, and it will show you care.

5) Show affection: are you guilty of complacency in your relationship? Maybe you both are, and it can seem stale. Bring back the romance and show your partner some affection. Grab their hand when out shopping or surprise them with a romantic night in! Flowers and candy may seem like kids' stuff, but they work!

Every relationship is different, and none are perfect no matter what you are told. Quality relationships are what we all crave, but sometimes we must put the effort in. If you feel the relationship is worth saving, you will know the best ways to make sure that happens.

How to Avoid Manipulation in General

First, you must realize that everybody can be a jerk now and then, but some people seem incapable of being anything else. Toxic people are often incapable of change, so they should be avoided. If you know that certain people are hell-bent on making you feel miserable, why are you still in contact with them?

Get rid of people who are Dr Jekyll and Mr Hyde type personalities. We are all prone to mood swings, but when someone is completely lovely to you one day and then prickly or bad-tempered the next day, they could have a toxic personality. If they refuse to answer your calls or disappear from your life for days on end with no apparent reason, then they are messing with your emotions. This type of manipulation is not acceptable, and they should be cut from your life.

Be Aware of Your Own Feelings

When we experience manipulation or emotional abuse, we are often left with feelings that are hard to define. We worry too much about what the other person is feeling and what we have done to upset them. Take the time to reflect on your own feelings for a change. Are you experiencing guilt or shame about your actions? Why should you feel bad about someone else's behavior?

The truth is that reasonable, balanced, emotionally stable people often care more about being decent to others than they do about their feelings. Stop doing that and listen to the alarm bells ringing in your head. You have no reason to be feeling shame or guilt. Start feeling angry about how you have been treated and realize you have done nothing wrong.

Become a Good Listener

There is a distinct difference between someone trying to manipulate you and someone who is trying to get you to see their point of view. We can be too defensive if we have experienced manipulation in the past. Open your ears and try to understand what the other person is trying to tell you. If they are prone to using generalizations and blanket statements that are designed to squash your views, then call them out on it.

Narcissists don't want to hear your nuances, and they will refuse to acknowledge them. If all you can hear is black and white illogical terms, then walk away. You should state the reason for your departure. Tell them your time is too precious to listen to their "broken record" style of rhetoric.

Avoid Triangulation

Do you have a certain friend who will repeatedly tell you what other people are saying about you? They will tell you it's for your own good and you need to know the truth about how people see you. They love to report back falsehoods about what third parties are saying. This is one way that manipulators try and draw you in. They present themselves as the only trustworthy person in your life.

This method is known as "triangulation" and should be avoided at all costs. You should realize that the third party in the drama is just as much a victim as yourself. Try reversing the situation and join forces with the third party to turn the tables on the manipulating party.

Improve Your Frame Control

What is your "frame control?" Put simply; it is how you react to an interaction. Life is full of interactions, and how you view them is how you control your frame. They can be affected by time, location, intent, and natural flow. A strong frame requires a strong intention. You should know your mind and demonstrate to others that you are not easily swayed.

For instance, take the example of a salesman and customer. The customer has the intention of finding out a price without buying a product as he wants to explore other options. The salesman has the frame of selling the customer something no matter what. The individual with the strongest frame control will achieve their objective.

Frame Strengthening Exercises

If you feel your frame may be susceptible and needs work, then try these frame strengthening exercises. Just like regular muscles, your mind needs a workout every now and then.

1) Stick to a list: if you find the lure of the supermarket too difficult to ignore, try this simple task. Make a list and don't buy anything else. If you are determined to eat healthily, you can be distracted by a well-placed bag of chips! Use frame control to stick to essentials.

2) Make someone smile every day: when you have a strong frame, people want to be with you. If you can make people smile with your personality, you are halfway there. Nobody is suggesting you turn into a standup comedian but try being amusing. Consider the goal of making one person per day smile.

3) Go to sleep on time: have you ever outframed yourself at bedtime? You know you have a busy day tomorrow, and you should be asleep by 11 pm, but it's way past midnight, and you're still giving yourself ten more minutes before you go to bed. Decide on your bedtime and stick to it.

4) Join an acting class: if you want to become a force of nature, then take lessons from professionals! An acting class will help you to project your voice, use your mannerisms to get your meaning across and hold a strong frame. Acting is all about becoming a different person for a fixed time. If you want to be a believable consummate actor, then take a class.

5) Have life goals: people with strong frames tend to have set goals in life. Those with weaker frames will tend to drift. If you have well-defined goals in life, you can discard trivialities. Become more focused and believe you can achieve whatever you set out to do. Set goals in career, relationship, health, and spiritual matters to become a well-rounded individual with an awesome frame.

The importance of your frame can't be stressed enough. If you have a confident, optimistic frame of mind, you will recognize potential psychological attacks. You will also learn how to analyze what others are saying to you and discard trivial matters.

The bottom line is that we are all subject to PSYOPS every day. You will know what your weaknesses are and how to deal with them. There is no one quick fix to rid your life of toxic people, but a combination of methods will help you to live a healthier and happier life.

Conclusion

Thank you for reading *Psychological Warfare: The Ultimate Guide to Understanding Human Behavior, Brainwashing, Propaganda, Deception, Negotiation, Dark Psychology, and Manipulation*. Now you know the dangers of psychological warfare and the prevalence of it in society. Knowledge is power, and knowing how to deal with people can also be empowering.

Unless you plan on living in a cave for the rest of your life, you will have social interactions, and knowing how to navigate them is a key ingredient for success. You are also now better equipped to decipher between what is real and what is false news and to recognize the use of propaganda. Good luck with your newfound knowledge—use it well!

Part 2: Deception

An Essential Guide to Understanding How Machiavellian People Can Hide the Truth and Use their Knowledge of Human Behavior to Manipulate, Negotiate, and Persuade

Introduction

You are most likely reading this because you're curious about "dark psychology." But what does it even mean? Is it some form of dark magic possessed only by a few people well versed in the art of controlling others? Or is it more like a Harry Potter thing with the soul-sucking, happiness-draining dementors? In this book, you will finally get your questions about dark psychology answered with clarity.

Dark psychology is the science and art of using mind control and manipulation to get what you want. Where psychology is about learning about human behavior and how people generally interact with one another, dark psychology focuses more on coercion, persuasion, motivation, and manipulation tactics.

Already, you might wonder whether or not you would want to "manipulate" anyone, and whether you should even be reading this book. If this is you, it would be wise to go ahead and read this. The world is not all flowers and roses, and you'd be doing yourself a huge favor learning about the dark triad, especially Machiavellians, who this book is primarily about. Having this awareness will prepare you for any eventual meeting with one of these people.

Some people read books like this because they would like to learn how to manipulate everyone around them. If this is you, here is a note: Be sure that you use everything you learn here for the greater good.

Machiavellianism is one of three manifestations of dark psychology or the dark triad. The thing about the dark triad is that, often, possessing these traits is a great predictor of troublesome relationships and a blatant disregard for law and order. The narcissist is the one who displays grandiosity and egotism unparalleled, along with a distinct lack of empathy. The psychopath is a charmer, your friendliest friend, and often impulsive and selfish, with no capacity for remorse or empathy. Finally, there is the Machiavellian who is a master of deception and has no qualms exploiting people if it means they get what they want, unfettered by such frivolous things as "morality," which regular folks hold dear.

Unlike other books on this subject, this one is up to date and easy to understand. If you are a beginner—just learning about dark psychology—you will find this a friendly guide on Machiavellian ways. If you're well versed in these matters, you will very likely learn new things. This book is written in a straightforward, easy-going style, so you won't struggle with the concepts.

Throughout the pages, you will come to understand the true nature of a Machiavellian. You will learn how they are so skilled at deception and how they use what they know about you to persuade and control you.

What you're about to learn is extremely potent and should be used only for good purposes. What you do with this knowledge, in the end, is entirely up to you.

Chapter One: Introduction to Dark Psychology

There are people you run into every day for who persuasion and manipulation is an elevated art form. These people are often experts at wearing masks from the moment they step out into the world because if the world were to see what truly lies beneath their masks . . . well, it probably wouldn't bode very well for them.

The Dark Psychology Triad

Here is what makes up this triad:

- Narcissism
- Psychopathy
- Machiavellianism

The narcissist is the most self-centered person you will ever meet, has no empathy, and believes that everything about them is larger than life itself. Dare to challenge this thought process, and they will make you regret it.

The psychopath is ever charming. This would not be a problem if they weren't also completely lacking in empathy—like the narcissist. They are very impulsive and have no remorse. You probably know the saying, "Some people just want to watch the world burn?" Well, "some people" are basically psychopaths.

Now the Machiavellian. No one lies better than this member of the dark triad. They do not just lie for the heck of it, either; they'll tell whatever tales they must if it means getting people to do their bidding. They have no morals, and for them, people are simply toys to be manipulated as they see fit. The Machiavellian sees nothing wrong with lying if it means they get their way. Don't bother trying to preach them a sermon; a Machiavellian understands how humans think and feel and uses this knowledge to their advantage. However, you most likely will be unaware of their complete grasp of human nature. This is part of what makes them so effective in their tactics . . . and dangerous.

Manipulation: More Common than You Realize

You may think that these people exist on the fringes. Odds are, you won't run into someone so manipulative. However, this manipulation goes on every day. Sure, you may not be the specific target of a Machiavellian, but more people than you realize have to deal with their lies.

In fact, you will find that manipulation happens all around you. You'll find it in sales letters, commercials, Internet ads, radio ads, television, newspapers—the works. As a parent or guardian, you will have to deal with this sort of behavior from teenagers as they discover who they really are and try to figure out the best way to get what they want and express their autonomy.

Don't be alarmed, but more often than not, dark manipulation and persuasion techniques are used by the people nearest and dearest to you, the ones you love and trust.

Everyday Manipulative and Persuasive Tactics

In case you still want to hold on to the notion that you are not a witness to manipulation and persuasion each day, perhaps a simple list of such tactics will help you see the truth.

1. *Giving the silent treatment.* You may have experienced or witnessed this for yourself, where someone deliberately gives you the cold shoulder, won't speak to you, and even goes to great lengths to avoid running into you.

2. *Love bombing.* Giving compliments and showing love and affection only to get someone to soften up enough to ask them for a favor.

3. *Denying love.* Ever heard of a spouse or lover withholding affection from their significant other to get them to apologize or do something they wouldn't otherwise?

4. *Lying.* Telling flat-out or "white" lies and embellishing stories here and there to seem more interesting.

5. *Boxed-in choices.* The manipulator gives you only a couple of options, which serve to keep you from realizing that there are other options you can choose besides the ones they've presented.

6. *Manipulating semantics.* Here, the manipulator uses words that can easily mean a million different things. When you confront them later on, they tell you they meant something entirely different from what you thought.

7. *Reverse psychology.* The manipulator asks you to do something, knowing fully well you'd rather do the opposite of what they ask, and expecting you to follow through on your own "original" thought.

Perhaps you are starting to realize how common manipulation is, or you may realize you have even used a few of these tactics yourself. The point is to let you know it is not too hard to fall prey to these techniques, no matter who or where you are. It happens at work, in friendships, families, relationships, media, politics, religion . . . everywhere.

Now, this is not to say that everyone who uses any of these tactics is necessarily a part of the dark triad. Sometimes, people are unaware of what they're doing and how wrong and unethical these methods are. Children are very impressionable, so many people learn these tactics just from observing adults or strong influences in their lives. Some people learned these manipulation techniques in the process of living their teenage lives. Some people learn these tricks later in life and usually coincidentally, not out of a need to control others. They used a technique and got their desire handed to them on a silver platter, so they continue with these methods to make it further along in life.

Additionally, some get actual training in the art of manipulation and persuasion. You can use programs to learn how to get your way most of the time, using tricks that are often very unethical. This is especially the case when it comes to making sales or being involved in the marketing world. With these dark tactics, they can drum up desire and literally flip a switch in your mind that tells you you have absolutely got to have the product du jour. You think you got a good deal when really, they're the ones who rake in most of the money and benefits.

Meet Possible Members of the Dark Triad

Just what kind of people are a part of this group?

Politicians. Though there are some good ones, many often use dark manipulation tactics to get people to see things their way. They do and say what they must to get people on their side. Some convince themselves it's for the greater good; others are conscious of being in it only for themselves.

Attorneys. Some attorneys will stop at nothing to win a case. They'll use dark tactics to sway things their way, and they won't feel a shred of remorse over being unethical.

Leaders. Several leaders have mastered the art of dark persuasion. They use the most devious methods to make sure their followers fall in line and continue to bend over backward to deliver better and better performance.

Salespeople. If you've ever read a sales letter, you probably think you're merely reading a bunch of words advertising a particular product, and there is nothing more going on. However, a lot is going on when you consider the subtext of these sales letters' messages. They're deliberately written to trigger primal emotions in you that make you act just the way the writer wants you to.

Public speakers. Public speaking is another arena where you'll see dark persuasion thriving. The public speakers use these techniques to get their audience hooked and make sure that they keep coming back for more and spending more money on the next tier product and the next event.

Generally, selfish people will also use these techniques because what better way to make sure they always get what they want? As far as they are concerned, everyone else can burn.

It may seem as though this book is glorifying the process of using dark methods to manipulate everyone and get your way, and it may seem like that is really the best way to go. However, in the end, going dark is never worth it. When people and businesses get into these techniques, over time, there is a lack of trust. You can only fool people for so long before they wise up to your game.

A Matter of Ethics

So how can you tell when you are ethical as you attempt to persuade or motivate someone? It is really as simple as assessing your intentions. You must be honest in your assessment. You have to figure out why you're trying to persuade or motivate someone to take action. Are you trying to help them? There is nothing wrong with helping yourself in the process, as long as whatever your end game is, it's mutually beneficial for all parties involved.

A good rule of thumb is to make sure that you aim to create a win-win situation no matter what you are doing. You must not goad yourself into assuming something is really good for the other party just to assuage your conscience. It needs to be a true win.

What Drives the Darkness?

There are many reasons why people with dark triad personalities do what they do. Sometimes, it is a matter of being accepted. For others, it's about getting ahead in life, becoming more successful in work, or getting paid a lot of money. Others still are simply in it for the glory of power and the feeling of being in control of everything and everyone. Some are driven by their love for religion or political leanings. There is a fair number who are the way they are on account of a psychiatric disorder.

The thing to understand about these dark predators is that they can be anyone—from any country, race, religion, or economic standing. So, do not be quick to dismiss your seemingly kind and charismatic preacher or leader or philanthropist simply because you expect they want the best for everyone, more than most.

No One is Blameless

The truth is: Everyone can express dark triad traits. They have the ability to take it so far, past the point of no return, where they only ever see everyone around them as prey and hunt for no reason other than because they can.

You should know what this is referring to. Sometimes you have that one, wicked, dark thought that comes out of nowhere, sometimes forcing you to ask, "Where did that come from?" This should not worry you, though, because most people never act out those thoughts. For the narcissists, psychopaths, and Machiavellians, not only do they express those dark inclinations, but they also draw a lot of pleasure and satisfaction from doing the thought(s). They also think that the people who fall prey to their antics deserve it since they were too naive and got swept up in their manipulations. They actually become addicted to their predatory behavior.

Today, with the advent of the Internet and the world shrinking into a global village on account of social media, it is very important to become aware of these dark inclinations that certain members of the human race harbor. When you also factor in the anonymity that the Internet grants every cybercitizen, you can surely see how, more than ever, people with dark personalities can thrive and go beyond the limits they otherwise had before social media and the Internet existed.

The rest of this guide focuses on "the Machiavellian" and how they wield deception ever so skillfully against regular folk to achieve their devious desires. Having established that monsters are masquerading as regular people, now turn your attention to the matter of deception. What counts as deception? Who do people consider deceptive, and under what situations is that deception malevolent, if at all?

Chapter Two: What is Deception?

Deception is the act of misleading people. It is about keeping the truth hidden, or propagating ideologies and beliefs that are the furthest thing from the truth, usually to get some advantage or advancement. There are many ways that deception can play out, including outright propaganda, distraction—typically in conjunction with sleight of hand—concealment, dissimulation, or camouflage. Deception also includes self-deception. It's all about presenting false claims as truth.

Deception inevitably will be discovered. Upon discovery, it's inevitable that the deceived party feels betrayed and would think twice about trusting the deceiver ever again. When people relate with one another, there is a natural expectation that there will be honesty and transparency. For this reason, deception is the desecration of the rules of a relationship, which are held sacred and dear to humans.

For the most part, if you think about it, you expect that lovers, family, friends, coworkers, and even strangers will be honest. The only time you really expect dishonesty is if you have had to deal with a traumatic experience that leaves you with your guard up, or if you have witnessed or heard of a person's propensity for dishonesty. With that being said, there's still a fair bit of deception that happens, even between you and the one who keeps the other side of your bed warm every night.

Kinds of Deception

Deception comes in various forms, from distortions and omissions of truth to making dishonest claims designed to get the other person to take whatever action you want them to—often at their own expense. Deception can also play out not just in words but in actions as well. Say you want to buy a pair of shoes. You inspect one shoe out of the pair, when some other shopper stands by you, picks up the other, and inspects it. In the process, they may make a face that communicates disgust or dislike, puts the shoe down, and walks away.

Having done that, if you are not someone who is particularly certain of your style, or if you weren't sure about that shoe initially, you will probably begin to see everything wrong with the shoe on account of the way they reacted. So, you just might decide the shoes are not worth the money, put it down, and walk away. Seconds later, the person swings by and decides they actually do like the shoes and buy them. This is a very basic example of how deception can play out in action.

Here are some misleading claims. For instance, a company that manufactures fruit juice may write on the can, "Made with 100 percent real fruit," knowing fully well that most people will see that and decide, "Wow, that's gotta be healthy. I'm buying it." In truth, it could be that the "100 percent real fruit" actually makes up only about three percent of the can. After all, the label says, "made with," not "made of." A more discerning buyer will turn to see the ingredients, which will no doubt begin with "Water, sugar . . ." and find that really what they have is a can full of sugar, preservatives, coloring, and flavoring, with just a pinch of "100 percent real fruit."

Sure, the company claim what they made is the truth; however, technically, the fact is that it will lead the buyers to draw false conclusions.

To cut to the meat of the matter, here are the various forms of deception people deal with every day:

1. *Lies.* You're given information that is completely different from the truth.

2. *Concealments.* You're deliberately only given a bit of the picture. The deceiver will leave out critical bits of information that will put what they're saying in the proper context, or they will act in ways that will muddy the relevant facts.

3. *Equivocations.* You are fed very contradictory statements or vague, indirect statements instead of an actual answer.

4. *Understatements.* The deceiver deliberately downplays the most significant parts of the truth to trick you, minimizing their importance.

5. *Exaggerations.* The deceiver will tell you the "truth"—only it's an incredibly stretched version and overstates or magnifies bits that will keep you in the dark.

6. *Misinterpretations.* The deceiver will give you the truth but deliberately misinterpret it.

It is important to note the motive behind the deception. In their paper "Interpersonal Deception Theory," Buller and Burgoon (1996, 202 - 242) identify the following motivations for acting deceptively.

- Instrumental motives: The deceiver lies to keep their resources safe or avoid being punished.

- Relational motives: The deceiver lies to keep their relationships strong or establish new, beneficial ones.

- Identity motives: The deceiver is motivated by the need to protect their image or save face.

You might be tempted to say from your lofty, mighty steed, "Well, I never deceive anyone. I keep everything honest and above board." Well, do you really? Think about the time someone apologized for nail clippings, and you replied, "Oh, it's okay, no big deal," knowing fully well that each *clip* sound brought you a step closer to blowing your lid. Or the time when a friend was feeling down in the dumps about something, and so, desperate to have your good buddy back to their old, cheerful self, you gave a compliment you did not mean, or told them something wasn't their fault—even though you both knew it was. The point is that all sorts of people engage in deception. The trouble is a matter of degree.

In fact, you can almost make a case that deception is something that happens, even in nature. Now take a look at the defense mechanism of camouflage, for instance. The sole purpose of the chameleon is to change its color to match the environment around it. The purpose of the wallaby's coloring is to match its surroundings and make sure they are safely hidden from prey. Even the military uses camouflage uniforms and gear, for this same purpose of appearing inconspicuous, as nothing more than part of the furniture.

Deception also happens in the form of disguise. To disguise something is to make it appear to be someone else or something else entirely. Celebrities, when they need to do everyday things and do not want the paparazzi trailing them everywhere, will often wear disguises or go incognito. A disguise can go beyond just looks. Sometimes, there is a change in natural speech patterns, voice, walking pace, and so on. An example of a disguise is Sherlock Holmes, who would often try to appear as someone else so no one would recognize him.

The disguise can also play out in abstract ways, where it is ideas that are disguised as something other than what they really are. This typically happens in government and the political space as a whole. In other words, this disguise is propaganda. You may have heard the phrase "Peacekeeping mission" and wondered why anyone got shot if the real goal was to keep the peace. Or you may hear the phrase "protective custody" being bandied about when really what is going on is government-sanctioned kidnapping.

What other way can deception occur? Dazzle. Dazzling has the effect of leaving the other party too confused to see the truth or take in the more significant stuff. Take a debate between two high schoolers from different schools. One presents logical facts; the other simply "make their points" by asking rhetorical questions after rhetorical questions, barely giving the audience and the judges any time to think critically and realize that they weren't making actual points. Naturally, the dazzling debate team wins, even though they shouldn't have. Another example of this dazzling deception is when an octopus shoots out a cloud of black ink, so predators do not see it when it escapes.

Who Uses Deception?

People who are defiant by nature. With these people, they are more obvious about their deception. They're often very rebellious and will do all they can to get away with a lot of bad stuff without any consequences. Think of your teen who thinks they're smarter than you and tries to escape the repercussions of their actions. The truth is that there is no point in doing things and getting away with it if they don't have any form of acknowledgment for the feat. For this reason, it is easy to spot them being deceptive.

People with deceptive personality traits. They are not the same as those with full disorders. Typically, this kind of person is passive-aggressive. Often, they do not realize that they're seen as deceptive people. For instance, if you have this sort of person as part of a project, and they really don't want to be involved in it, they might procrastinate or conveniently forget to do important things. When you do confront this individual, they are quick to appeal to your emotions, rather than meet you on a logical level about why they're acting how they are, and how you might both arrive at a solution.

People with a personality disorder. Whether it is someone with a narcissistic personality disorder, obsessive-compulsive disorder, or someone who's paranoid, borderline, or histrionic, the fact remains that there's an inaccurate perception of reality in their minds. They will often try to make you a part of their delusional world.

These people are often motivated by a deep fear of rejection, abandonment, or failure, as well as insecurities. They may have experienced some traumatic event in their childhood that has contributed to them turning out the way they have. For these people, they do their best to keep all this fear and insecurity hidden from everyone, and that is why they will craft their own version of events and rope you into believing it all.

People who fall under the dark triad. These sociopaths and psychopaths are very well advanced in their deception tactics and adept at reading everyone through subtext, body language, and simple observation. Being able to read people with ease, they know what to say or do and how to say or do it so that their prey feels a false sense of security with them.

With the people in this group, there is no form of empathy, kindness, or shred of goodness in them. They are completely comfortable with even taking advantage of those that are nearest and dearest to them. As far as they are concerned, the end justifies the means. If they perceive that the only way to get what they want is to get rid of you, they will do so without hesitation and won't look back. They're experts at wielding abuse in subtle, insidious ways, and often, the victim is hardly ever aware of what is going on until it's too late.

The Truth About Deception

Deception is a prevalent part of people's lives, and it plays a useful part, like it or not. However, not all lies are motivated by personal gain at the expense of another. Most lies people tell are for others' sake, just to make sure that everyone can relate without a hitch. That being said, no one likes to feel like they have just been had.

So, if everyone lies, what is the difference between a Machiavellian and an ordinary Jane or Joe? Motive. Studies also show that deception might be a good thing. In a Philosophize This! Podcast on Machiavellianism, it becomes pretty obvious that Machiavelli was not necessarily postulating that everyone becomes deceptive for the sake of it. The theory is that he only wrote *The Prince* to make it clear that while it is fine to want to uphold moral values like honesty and forthrightness in all aspects of life, it is especially impossible for leaders in politics or in general to be honest if they intend to have any form of stability and peace during their administration.

While casting Machiavelli's intentions in this light does make what he wrote appear less villainous, the fact remains that there are Machiavellians who are not simply trying to rule. They are out for number one, and they will mow down anyone to make it happen.

Chapter Three: Defining Machiavellianism

This chapter begins with the origin of the word "Machiavellianism." Niccolo Machiavelli was a Renaissance writer who wrote *The Prince*. The book is about the various techniques that leaders need to use if they want to have a loyal following and ensure order and stability in the land. It was less about doing what was morally right, and more about doing what needed to be done, no matter the cost.

According to Machiavelli, there are two ways to rule. One way is by the law and supposedly brings peace. The other is by brute force. When the first way does not work out, the leader will have to turn to the second way. As such, the wisest ruler will do well not to make promises with the intent to follow through, especially if those promises are actually not in their best interests.

The Machiavellian view of people is that they are all intrinsically bad, and for this reason, the wise leader would do well to deceive them when they must since the people themselves are not particularly trustworthy. Machiavelli states that people are often easily swayed by whatever it is they need at the moment, so it is easy to use these needs to have them dancing to your tune. In his words,

"He who seeks to deceive will always find someone who will allow himself to be deceived."

Machiavelli postulated that the leader must adhere to the laws, ethics, and principles in place when ruling over a state. However, when needed, the leader must also be able and willing to hold on to their power by lying and being cunning. In other words, rather than make like the Red Queen and yell, "Off with their heads," the leader would be wise to use flattery and kindness, even if they do not mean it. It would serve them better to seem gracious, kind, honest, and even religious. Machiavelli says it would be best to have these virtues but be prepared to dump them at a moment's notice when circumstances dictate that would be the best course of action.

Machiavellianism and Psychology

Florence Geis and Richard Christie were the very first researchers to consider Machiavellianism regarding psychology, rather than politics. They described it as a behavior, trait, or attitude. Thanks to these American researchers, Machiavellianism is not a trait that only applies to politicians and leaders, and it doesn't mean the same thing as having an authoritarian personality. It is also not simply a psychopathological matter. Even the most ordinary folk can think like Machiavellians, depending on the situations they are faced with.

Machiavellian Traits

Trait #1: Manipulation. As far as the Machiavellian is concerned, there is nothing wrong with being manipulative. They are at home with deception and trickery. They are ever on the prowl to gain something by being manipulative and deceitful. They're incredibly selfish, insensitive, and downright evil when dealing with others.

Despite how much they absolutely love to manipulate people, Machiavellians always tread carefully. They will only ever strike when they see an opportunity to make trouble, get what they want, and get away with it with no one the wiser.

The Machiavellian always has some justification for the things that they do. They will rationalize their most dastardly deeds to no end and will make you believe that in their shoes, you will more than likely have done the same thing. They have all sorts of weapons in their arsenal when it comes to their deception. They will intrude, flatter you, act like they're very cooperative, and do all they can to maneuver themselves right where they need to be to rip the rug out from under you.

The Machiavellian is not a psychopath, though—as they are on the darkest end of the dark triad. Yes, a Machiavellian is both incredibly insensitive and callous, but the psychopath never has a guilty conscience about what they do. As for Machiavellians, they're not so aggressive. They would rather act with tact.

One thing you should know about the Machiavellian or the Mach is that they have a slew of methods to deceive people. In a study by Geis, Christie, and Nelson (1970, pp. 285 - 313), the subjects had been asked to find hidden objects in a picture, while the researcher noted the amount of time it took to find them all. After they were done, the subjects took on the researcher's role and gave the next set of subjects the same test they'd just finished. When they were through, the researcher asked them to distract and disturb other subjects who were still working on their assignments, to keep them from finishing on time. It was left to the subjects' discretion what methods they used to keep the other people distracted.

This study showed that participants with the highest Mach scores on a Mach test had a diverse and wide range of methods to influence non-Mach subjects. They would lie, withhold information, and ask questions that served to confuse and were completely irrelevant when you looked beneath the surface. They also frequently sighed, hummed, whistled a tune, tapped their pencil repeatedly against the desk, and continued to rearrange all the objects they found on the desk. The Mach's were the ones who came up with the most inventive ways to use such distracting techniques to achieve their goal.

You would be hard-pressed to find a better liar than a Machiavellian. In a study by Azizli et. al, Lies and crimes: Dark Triad, Misconduct, and High-Stakes Deception. Personality and Individual Differences (2016, pp. 34 - 39), carried out to test just how likely the subjects were to lie, the participants were given questionnaires meant to gauge how likely they'd get into deception, particularly the kind with high stakes. In all the scenarios presented in the questionnaires, Machiavellians were clearly at home with deception in all forms. However, they were very eager to be a part of high-stakes deception, even more than the garden-variety psychopath is likely to lie.

All of this being said, the Mach does not feel the need to lie all the time, and they are not always necessarily smooth about it. They do not think it is absolutely a must to tell lies every time their lips start moving. For them, it's simply that lying is necessary to get ahead, especially as the world is full of unreliable people as far as they're concerned—never mind that they probably caused these people to act in unreliable ways, to begin with. For the Machiavellian, when the truth will not give them what they want, the lie is the logical choice.

Trait #2: Amorality. Machiavellians are completely fine with being amoral and disrespecting ethics. For them, it is all about what matters to them, and if there's a moral or ethical rule in between them and what they want, you can bet your bottom dollar they're not going to let that get in their way. They would rather have injustice than fail.

The Mach will continue to test you, provoke you, see where your boundaries lie and how they can break them. The very moment the Mach spots weakness in you, they are going to pounce. If there is money to be made, they're fine with ignoring ethics and are even more eager to do whatever amoral thing is necessary. The fact that the Mach never allows social conventions to control them is what makes them the best manipulators.

Trait #3: Cynicism. You will never find anyone more cynical than a Mach. They believe that you can never trust what anyone says or what they do. They'll often assume that people have the worst intentions, that they're all liars and schemers, and therefore should never be confided in or trusted. For the Machiavellian or Mach, they must ever remain vigilant in case someone decides to take advantage of them. In fact, this often leads to them taking advantage of other people so that they can be the first one to be deceitful. This sort of thinking is how the Machiavellian excuses their behavior. After all, why be kind or honest when the other person is most definitely not.

The Machiavellian sees people as being dishonest even when it comes to themselves, holding an impression of goodness that is really not there. They believe that this false knowledge of self is what makes their victims even more vulnerable.

With this inherent cynicism, a Mach can cause an imbalance in power between you and them. They do not consider you an equal but think of you as inferior and open to manipulation—since they believe they have a firmer grasp on your behavior than you do. In a way, they are right. Many people are driven to do the things they do on account of external factors, rather than because they've decided to take action independently. This is what allows the Mach to step into your life, as an external force, and bend you according to their will to gain something from you.

Trait #4: Coldness. The Mach is reserved and cold. They are indifferent to everything. If you want a lesson in detaching yourself from emotions, the Mach will be the best tutor you could ever have. They do not care how you feel and would rather be rational about everything. They are more about their goals than they are about people, and they pay attention to the things that will benefit them while completely disregarding how you feel about their methods or what they're doing to you.

The Mach can think about all the options in a very cool, detached way. This is advantageous to them because no matter what situation they find themselves in, they know just how to control it. They put their goal front and center, sift through all the information they're getting, and figure out the best options and strategies to allow them to achieve their end. They are not concerned with whether your reaction to their methods is one of approval or disapproval; this person is only concerned with doing what they think is best for them.

You can never distract the Mach with your emotions, no matter how intense or terrible they are. Machiavellianism exists on a spectrum. With a high Mach, you can never get in their way when it comes to gaining a better position, promotion, or making more money. A low Mach cares a lot more about the people in their lives, both at work and at home, and this leaves them in a much more vulnerable position since they do not believe that the end justifies the means.

Trait #5: No empathy. No matter what you are going through, the Mach is both unable and unwilling to consider how you feel or walk in your shoes. They lack empathy. Whether you feel pain or joy, the Mach can't relate to it. They're not the most helpful or selfless people, either, so don't expect them to reach out a hand when you're dangling over the end of a cliff—unless, of course, saving you is a means to an end for them. They don't believe in promoting others and would rather keep you under their thumb than give you a leg up. If you're working with a Mach, you have to do things the way they want it. Don't try to get creative—you'll just be asking for a world of hurt.

The Mach is not big on cooperation, and this is no surprise since they have zero empathy. Even if they've been in your particularly difficult position before and know how inconvenient it is, they just can't be bothered. The last thing they will ever do is allow themselves to cooperate or relate to the pain you feel since this will only keep them from doing what they must. This is what makes the Mach such a skilled, cold-blooded manipulator.

Trait #6: High toxicity. The only thing more toxic than dealing with a Machiavellian is taking a bath in a vat of radium. No matter how much you try to be positive and upbeat, the Machiavellian is like a dark cloud, ever willing and happy to rain on your parade. They are incredibly negative and toxic. Being with them often leaves you feeling drained and beyond overwhelmed.

Trait #7: Narcissism. The Mach is more than likely a narcissist. They have extremely narcissistic traits, like only caring about themselves and having a complete disregard for others' interests. They are anything but generous, thoughtful, or mindful of other people around them. If it is not about the Mach, it has no weight or meaning.

The Mach's Empathy

When it comes to empathy, there are two kinds: cold and hot. Cold empathy is mostly something you know on a logical level. You understand the way other people think. You understand what it is they might feel given certain conditions. You get why they act the way they do, and you understand the evolution of events with each person around you. You use cold empathy to grasp how others would feel or react if you were to take a certain line of action.

You use hot empathy to deal with and resonate with other people on an emotional level. However, the Mach does not care about trying to establish this connection. They have cold empathy but don't bother with hot. The reason they need cold empathy is simple: sometimes, they will need to make you believe they truly care so that they can get what they need from you.

Signs of Machiavellianism

Here is a quick list of signs that you are dealing with a Machiavellian and need to watch your back:

1. They have a laser-like, single-minded focus on *their* interests and ambitions.

2. They are confident in everything they do and say.

3. They are incredibly charming.

4. They are very keen on power and money but display a marked indifference when it comes to relationships.

5. They often resort to flattery.

6. They are at home with deception and lies when they deem it necessary.

7. They are unwilling to think or believe the best about other people.

8. They are not big on values or morals.

9. They are comfortable with manipulating others when they have got to have their way.

10. They are rarely ever empathetic, and when they are, it almost seems manufactured.

11. They never let you know what their real intentions are.

12. They do their best not to get bogged down by emotions or commitments.

13. They do not believe in such things as good or people having a conscience.

14. They are at home with hurting other people to get what they want.

15. When you meet them, they seem really difficult to get to know, and they have an air of aloofness about them.

16. They are not shy about being promiscuous and will often have casual sex.

17. They are experts at reading other people and "reading the room."

18. They are not really warm when interacting with other people socially.

19. They might have serious trouble figuring out how they feel about things.

20. They do not have a grasp on the consequences of what they do and say.

The Machiavellian Scale

As mentioned, Machiavellianism exists on a spectrum. The Machiavellianism scale rates Machs from 0 to 100, using a series of questions in a test. Those who score above 60 are "high Machs," while those who score below 60 are "low Machs."

The low Mach is okay with showing others empathy. They are mostly trusting and honest in their interactions. For them, people are intrinsically good, and success means having good morals. If they are way too low on the Mach scale, that just makes them far too agreeable and submissive.

The high Mach is only all about number one. They are only concerned when something or someone seems to threaten their wellbeing. For them, they must employ deception in their day-to-day interactions. They don't care much for human goodness, because it doesn't exist as far as they're concerned. The Mach will never put themselves in a position where they have to depend on you or anyone else, because they think that is an incredibly foolish and naive thing to do. For them, power matters more than love and relationships. Everything else is meaningless.

Nature or Nurture?

At this point, you might be wondering: Is the Machiavellian born this way, or do they become this way? What is the actual origin of this trait? Would one really be a Machiavellian if they were an ordinary person who decided to read *The Prince* just so they can start acting like an actual Mach?

While Machiavellianism is a trait, it is not the only distinctive feature of a manipulative personality. As previously stated, when a person is truly Machiavellian, they will often score as a high Mach . . . unless they decide to deliberately score as a low Mach to fly under the radar—which is not unusual for these highly deceptive people. The thing is, for the most part, the rest will test as low Machs. This doesn't mean they are incapable of deception—it just means that manipulation and deception are not their baselines.

In the realm of politics, being a Machiavellian means that you are a cynic who will often be very calculating in the ways you acquire power and how you make sure that power never leaves your hands. In psychology, Machiavellianism is a trait that you obtain, where you look at all human interactions through the eyes of a cynic and nothing more. If you are a Mach, you'll know it because everything—as far as you're concerned—is a matter of win or lose.

To be clear, there is most likely some influence from genetics when it comes to whether or not someone is a Machiavellian, or whether they will be selfish, callous, and manipulative. That said, it is not entirely on nature; nurture also plays a part. While the genes may exist, the fact is that your experiences growing up, home life, and the way your parents raised you will most likely contribute to whether you will become a dreaded high Mach. You cannot expect someone who has gone through dozens of foster homes from the day they were born to emerge a regular, normal human being. It is not unheard of, but it's rare.

Science has found that some people are genetically predisposed to being psychopaths. However, even without the genes, if you have had a terrible start to the game of life, you are more likely to be affected, no matter how normal your brain structure is or how basic your genes. This is the same thing, whether it is narcissism, psychopathy, or Machiavellianism.

As for people who deliberately learn what it is like to be a Machiavellian so that they can apply these strategies in their lives, well, it's not hard to see why. This is not an endorsement of Machiavellianism, but it would be untrue to say that there are not specific situations where being a Mach would be advantageous. There are scenarios where even Machs on the lowest end of the spectrum will find themselves having to resort to Machiavellian methods to defend themselves or protect their space.

Say you are homeless and have to move in with a friend, but this friend proves themselves to be anything but a good one over time. They treat you like crap and make it seem to everyone else under that roof like you're a whole world of trouble, attacking you when no one else is watching, or when they won't get caught. You might find yourself backed into a corner where, in order to protect yourself till you move out, you start to act like a Machiavellian. You might deliberately withhold or skew information to get back at them or get more people on your side.

If you are dealing with a toxic work environment, you might find yourself doing anything and everything to get toxic colleagues off your back. You might tell lies to stop people from piling their responsibilities onto you. You might swoop in to claim credit for things that you didn't actually do as a way to warn off the offending colleagues who have made your life difficult. You might even start a few rumors. You do not want to do any of this, and you don't relish it at all, but you realize that to try to stay ethical and above board in such an environment is virtually impossible, as everyone around you would love to play pin the tail on the donkey and there are only so many pins you can take without going bonkers.

Chapter Four: How to Hide the Truth

It is time to talk about lies. Studies have shown that roughly 60 percent of people tell a lie every ten minutes or so. Now, this is not enough to say everyone lies. That being said, you have to agree that 60 percent is not a number you can easily ignore, especially when you put that percentage up against the entire populace in America. A study carried out by psychologist Robert S. Feldman of the University of Massachusetts in 2002, published in the Journal of Basic and Applied Social Psychology, demonstrated that it's hard for most people to have a conversation with others without telling a fib even once.

You might want to exclude yourself from this percentage of "liars," but sometimes you lie without even being aware of it. You tell many white lies—just because they are harmless doesn't mean that you're not a liar. Some lies you tell to make things go better in a relationship or make the other person feel better about themselves, which inevitably makes you more likable. However, it's still all deception in the end.

According to The Day America Told The Truth, a survey on mass morality by James Patterson and Peter Kim published by

Prentice Hall in 1991, our parents bore the brunt of our deception with 86 percent of us fooling them often, while we lied to siblings 73 percent of the time, friends 75 percent of the time, and lovers 69 percent of the time. Bear in mind that these percentages mostly pertain to lies about things that aren't really important and won't significantly affect how you relate with the people in your life.

Why People Lie

Who gets to judge a lie as meaningless, and by what criteria? Also, why do people even lie to begin with? The incredible thing about lies is that they are an inevitable part of society. Imagine a life where everyone only ever told the plain truth. Everyone would probably hate each other. Salespeople would sell nothing. Advertising and marketing would not exist. Your parents would wonder why in the heck they gave birth to you. Other people would look at you and your parents—or kids—as a lesson on why you should never have kids. Maybe the whole of humanity would become extinct.

Lying is something people have become so used to that they are now naturals at telling lies and being lied to. It is like a game everyone has agreed to play, and one of the rules is that you do not acknowledge you're playing it.

So, what is it exactly that prompts people to tell anything but the truth, even when under oath? To understand this urge, take a moment to really think about a world where everyone only ever tells the truth. If you cannot imagine it, you should watch the movie The Invention of Lying. Now, this once, be honest with yourself: Would you like to live in that world? Would you be able to handle the brutal truth about you and how people feel about you being flung in your face everywhere you go? Honestly?

Just because you tell lies does not make you a Machiavellian. It all comes down to intent. For the Machiavellian, lying is about having control and manipulating people to get what they want. So, why do ordinary people tell these "white" lies then?

1. *They want to fit in.* Everyone lies about the things they can do or have accomplished so that others think of them as being worthy of love and admiration. They lie because they want to be picked over the next person when they apply for "that" job or loan. They lie about having seen a movie or read a book they actually haven't because they just want the conversation to keep going without getting sidetracked, or because they're embarrassed to admit they're the one person on the planet who has not yet seen *Game of Thrones.* They tell these kinds of lies just to be accepted as part of a group and feel like they're a part of the whole, so they don't stick out like a sore thumb.

2. *They do not want to be punished.* From as young as two years old, people figured out that they could get away unscathed if they lied about something, with no punishment or consequences. Since then, people have learned to tell cover-up tales or one-liners to cover their hides and make it seem like their lapses in judgment or actions never happened.

3. *They do not want to hurt others.* One of the biggest reasons people lie is because they don't want others to be hurt by the truth. This happens a lot when you care for someone, as in a deep friendship or romantic connection. That said, lying in these situations can sometimes be a terrible idea. Say you are about to end a relationship for a very good reason. Maybe your partner is a slob or inconsiderate. It would be better to let them know so that they can do better in their next relationship, or they'll just remain as they are, never learning or growing. Sometimes, you also need people to be blunt with you. If you're not working as hard as you could, or if you did something wrong but were unaware of why it was wrong, in times like this, honesty really is the best policy.

4. *They want things to work out.* Whether you like it or not, lies have always played a very important role in getting the outcomes you prefer. You'll notice this when applying for work, as most people tend to embellish their résumés.   Certain professions necessitate using persuasion tactics to get people to buy some

product or service or vote for a particular candidate. Here, this is specifically referring to sales, advertising, marketing, and politics.

At this point, it should be pretty clear that lies are virtually unavoidable in people's day-to-day lives. They tell these harmless white lies to pave the way toward their hopes, goals, dreams, and better relationships with everyone around them.

Pathological Liars

If everyone is guilty of lying, what's the difference between you and a pathological liar? Pathological lying is a different beast altogether and is often a sign that the liar might have a mental health problem, like a personality disorder.

When you lie, you are making a statement that is not true so that you can deceive others to gain something from them, whether it's a better relationship or something material. Non-pathological lying is nothing unusual, and it doesn't mean you're not "all up there" when you lie to your kid about Santa. On the flip side, a pathological liar will tell lies compulsively. There is never any clear benefit or reason for them to lie—they just can't help themselves.

Pathological lies are told with zero motivation. Usually, when you lie, you have a solid reason. You do not want someone to be mad at you, or don't want to miss out on something, or want to help someone else feel better, or, or, or . . . With pathological lying, there is just no definite motivation, and you can't quite fathom why they'd bother to tell such a lie to begin with.

It is not particularly obvious whether or not the pathological liar is aware of their deception, or if they can even reason through their lies and figure out whether or not they are logical. Pathological lying is a very problematic thing, as it makes it really difficult to socialize with the liar, who has more likely than not shoved everyone away from them with all their lies.

Causes of Pathological Lying

Unfortunately, there has not been enough research carried out on this, so whatever causes pathological lying remains unknown. No one can tell if the lying is a condition all on its own, or if it's merely a symptom of an entirely different condition. The fact that telling compulsive lies is part of a few well-known conditions like personality disorders and factitious disorder makes it really difficult to figure out.

Factitious Disorder

Factitious disorder or Munchausen's syndrome is a unique condition where the affected individual will act like they are mentally or physically unwell when, in truth, they're actually fine.

There is also Munchausen's syndrome by proxy. In this condition, the affected individual will often lie about someone else having some disease or illness. For the most part, this syndrome affects mothers who will act like their kids are unwell and tell lies to their doctor about their child's condition.

It is unclear what causes this disorder, but here are a few theories: Childhood neglect or abuse, genetic or biological causes, substance abuse, low self-esteem, personality disorder, or depression.

To Lie or Tell the Truth: Gain or Lose?

In the short term, telling lies to get ahead can seem like a great shortcut to what you want in life. However, in the long run, you will find yourself losing a lot. The thing about lies is that sooner or later, the truth will become evident. When that happens, everything you have gained by lying will begin to crumble.

If you make a habit of telling lies, you will find that you are actually pushing away the people who would be critical to your success. No one wants to work with someone they cannot trust. Your relationships also suffer because everyone you love has no choice but to second guess everything you say and do—and that is assuming they're still sticking around you since lying makes you look terribly selfish and unappealing. Everyone abhors being deceived, and so it is only a natural inclination to want to get as far away from a known liar as possible.

Make a habit of being honest as often as you can. When you stay honest, you do not have to worry about never fulfilling your promises. You won't have to worry about doing something wrong that contradicts your story. You don't have to feel terrible about all the lies you have told, or worry that you're not the person you have led others to believe you are.

You might want to assume that there is nothing to the "small" lies you tell, but if you keep that up, sooner or later, you are going to start lying about the bigger things too. The things you do every day—your habits—often sculpt the person you will become tomorrow. Lying is also an incredibly slippery slope. You go from telling constant white lies to telling more consequential lies, cheating, and stealing from other people. This is how the Bernie Madoffs of the world are created.

Honestly, honesty is just a lot easier since you do not have to try to remember whom you told what, or worry about the little inconsistencies that are inevitable with each version of your tall tales; inconsistencies that make it easy for everyone to wise up to your dishonesty and deception.

How to Lie or Hide the Truth

To spot the Machiavellian, it would befit you to get into their minds and see just how they can do what they do so well. For this reason, included in this section is what to look out for.

1. *You must lie only when needed.* Do not lie unless you have to—which means you have something to gain. That is the difference between a skilled liar and a pathological one. The pathological liar will tell so many lies, and often that's what lands them in hot water. The expert liar will tell the truth and nothing but the truth—unless and until they have something to gain from lying.

2. *Work out your story.* You want to make sure you have figured out your story before you lie. Do not wait until the last minute to figure things out, because if you do, then you're going to get caught. You want to make sure you have thought through your story and addressed every objection that can be raised. When you've rehearsed your lie enough times, it makes it more difficult to catch you out.

3. *Lie with the truth.* Rather than go with an outright lie, you must, at least, bend the truth. The best lies are those that do not really lie. You should tell the truth in a way that allows people to take on a different impression than the one you would rather they didn't have.

4. *Understand your target.* You need to get into your target's head. In other words, all good liars are good communicators. They are experts at tapping into other people's thoughts and feelings and reading them accurately. You must be empathetic to your target because it is easy to tell exactly what they want to hear from you, and you won't stick your foot in it. It's not enough to think of how sound the logic of a lie is to you. You must also make sure you consider the point of view of your target. That way, you can easily cover your tracks.

5. *Keep your story straight.* Lying is hard. You need to be consistent about the details. If you have to take notes, take notes. The trouble with terrible liars is that they tell different stories to different people. This can confuse the liar and increase the likelihood that people will start talking—and they'll figure it out. So, keep your story straight, no matter who is asking you about it.

6. *Stay sharp.* You must be focused. You must commit to the story you are telling. If you're accused of lying, do not allow yourself to feel guilt or fear. If you do, those emotions will show on your face and in your mannerisms—they're a dead giveaway. Commit to the story. A great way to commit is to flip a switch in your head by actively recalling your new story as if it is exactly what happened. Convince yourself you're not a liar, and no one else can convince

you otherwise—even when you're smack dab in the middle of a lie. Enjoy the process of deception, of confusing your target. Whatever you do, do not feel ashamed or remorseful. If you can enjoy misleading them, then you're not likely to slip up. Beware the dreaded duper's delight, though. You don't want that small, secret smile to slip onto your face unless you're actually telling a funny or happy story.

7. *No giveaways.* Do you want to be a great liar? Then you need to be aware of what you are signaling nonverbally. You want to keep eye contact, but no more or less than you usually do in a conversation. You want to keep your body language and palms open, as this subconsciously communicates that you have nothing to hide. Keep your breathing even. Don't swallow. Don't scratch. Don't fidget. Don't let your voice go lower or higher than usual, and be mindful not to gesture more than usual.

8. *Crank it up.* When your target suspects you are lying, you have got to raise the bar emotionally. All the great liars are amazing at manipulating people. Double down on emotion. Alternatively, ask them to set aside their feelings and look at things logically for a moment, and then walk them through your brand of logic. The fact that you're using the word "logic" with them already prompts them to assume whatever next will come out of your mouth is the truth and nothing but. You can also distract them. If you are incredibly attractive, and you're fairly certain that they cannot help but notice it, play that up to your advantage. If you are a 40-year-old with a babyface, you can appeal to them by subtly playing up childlike innocence, especially if it's someone who feels a need to be in a position above you all the time.

9. *Push back.* Most regular people are not okay with lying and are just as uncomfortable with pointing fingers at others. As a liar, you can use this to your advantage. Notice the way politicians will aggressively respond to the accusations made against them. This aggression is not necessarily always what it seems. With this aggression, they turn their targets away from the actual issue, so that

they will have to regroup and have another go at accusing them—by this time, the politician will have sufficiently prepared for the next round of questions and accusations.

10. *Strike a deal.* Even if you are caught in a lie, you can escape the worst consequences by bargaining—as psychologists call it. What you want to do is reduce, soften, or totally eradicate all the feelings of responsibility for the lie you told. When you can reduce how accountable you are for the lies, as well as the anger and blame that result from your lies, you will be more likely to have an even better outcome than whatever lay in wait for you if you hadn't bargained.

Chapter Five: Learning Human Behavior

You cannot detect deception without understanding human behavior. This chapter details the various clues in human behavior that means deception is in play. While there are no specific clues that are exclusively tied to deception, there are clues that you can pay attention to regarding cognition and emotion.

For the most part, lies are often given away on account of the circumstances or factors around the lie, not necessarily by the liar's behavior. That said, sometimes behavior is all you have to go on to figure out whether or not you are being lied to about someone's actions or their intentions. Since the Machiavellian lies deliberately, it would not be a stretch to assume that there are some subtle signs in how they act that can give them away.

These are the questions that matter:

- Are there any clues that you can find when they tell lies?
- If there are clues, can you spot them with just your eyes, unassisted?
- Are these clues consistent all the time, regardless of the liar in question, the situation, or the culture in play?

- Assuming there are clues, is there a way to figure them out in real time, without using technology?

Wouldn't it be grand if every liar's nose magically grew an inch every time they told a lie? Unfortunately, this is not the case, and even science has not pinpointed a set of clues that apply to everyone, regardless of the situation and culture. The traditional clues of deception known to most folks, like fidgeting, stammering, avoiding eye contact, and so on, can happen for other reasons besides someone lying to you.

Learned Human Behaviors and Tics of a Liar

There is research on the detection of lies based on behavior, and you can broadly classify them into two categories:

- Cognitive clues involve the Machiavellian's memory and thoughts about what they are saying.

- Emotional clues involve the Machiavellian's feelings as they lie and their feelings around the subject of deception in general.

Cognitive Clues of Deception

There is a lot of effort that goes into the concealing, fabricating, or distorting information—much more effort than you would need simply to tell the truth. The Machiavellian will have to come up with stories about what did not actually happen, find ways to cover up what did happen and talk about things in such a way as to allow people to get whatever meaning they will out of their words.

There is also some effort involved in telling the truth when it is not exactly comfortable, as you'd need to find the most delicate way to put it so as not to offend the listener or make them feel bad. With telling uncomfortable truths, there are often clues, like more frequent disturbances in speech, the latency of speech, implausible or not so plausible ideas, much less involvement in terms of vocal and verbal communication, less time spent talking, and constant repetition of phrases and words, among other clues. The science also shows that there can be a change in nonverbal communication behaviors on account of all this effort. For instance, the usual hand and head movements that are made with speech will often give away when someone is lying versus telling the truth.

Another thing to consider when it comes to lies and cognition are the characteristics of naturalistic memory. When you have experienced an event, there are memory qualities, which are very clear as you describe those events, versus when you describe events that are not real. When you're telling a tall tale about something that never happened, your story often has more ambivalence and fewer details, and there is also no logical sequence of events, little to no plausibility a lot more in the way of negative statements, and less in the way of context.

The liar is not likely to admit to being forgetful, and they are not likely to make spontaneous adjustments or corrections to their stories. They may make more use of words describing negative emotions, and they also will do their best to distance themselves from the lie they're telling by referring to themselves as little as possible. The clues you can spot regarding the mental effort the liar uses appear to happen more as they deliver their lie. All clues about memory recall lie within the lie's context.

Be aware that not all lies require effort for everyone. Close-ended questions that require only "yes" or "no" answers are pretty easy to answer with a lie. An open-ended question that requires a liar to get into more detail is not as easy for them to answer if they intend to be dishonest. You can also expect that the cleverer the liar, the more persuasive they can be. This is especially so if they choose to use an event that actually did happen at some point in time as their alibi, rather than creating an entirely new one. For instance, they can tell you that they were doing their laundry at the time a crime happened when really, they only recall the day before—which is the actual day they did their laundry.

Emotional Clues

It is not uncommon for lies to cause emotions in the liar, from the expression of "duper's delight" at having successfully deceived someone to the anxiety and worry about getting caught, to feelings of immense guilt at having to lie about something. Typically, emotions will manifest in your facial expressions and the tone of your voice, and sometimes this is all you need to go on to reliably tell how someone feels at any given point in time.

Research shows that the facial expressions for specific emotions like contempt, anger, fear, happiness, disgust, distress, sadness, and surprise are universally recognized across all cultures and are pretty much the same worldwide. Depending on the stakes involved with the lie being told, there will often be more of these facial expressions and vocal tone changes. If it's a casual lie—meaning a lie most people tell all the time and without much thought—there won't be as much emotion in play.

Studies have also shown that a liar will often seem much more nervous than someone honest. They are not quite as pleasant concerning facial expressions. They speak with a higher pitch and a lot of tension, their pupils dilate, and they fidget. When the lie is about how feel, the liar will show how they're actually feeling in how they speak and the expressions on their face—regardless of how hard they try to cover up their emotions. Remember that while they will show these tells, they're very subtle and often brief.

The Liar's Targets

Again, lying happens every day. Many people tell lies, and often, it is really no picnic trying to work out when you're being played. Now, no one is exempt from being the sucker at any point in time, but the trouble is that some people are really easy to deceive and manipulate—in particular, people who are very:

1. Optimistic
2. Passive
3. Empathetic

The Empath

For the empath, there is no need to overthink when people seek support or help from them, or present themselves as vulnerable. The empath feels other people's joys and pains deeply, making them easy prey for the Machiavellian. They are incredibly adept at reading and sensing other people's emotions, and it is this remarkable skill that leaves them open to the Machiavellian's schemes. Not once does the empath assume that someone may be faking their tears. They just reach out to help and comfort them because that is who they are. Honestly, there's nothing wrong with being an empath as long as you're an empath who is careful.

The Passive or Naive

Those who are naive or passive are also pretty easy to fool as their thoughts are very simple, and they don't have enough judgment or experience to tell when they're being lied to. You would never catch them thinking twice when a liar puts one over them. To them, the world is a simple place, and there's no reason for anyone to want to complicate it by lying. So, when they're lied to, they don't even realize it.

The Optimist

Optimists are also vulnerable because they would rather assume the best of everyone. The trouble is: "everyone" also includes the liar. They look at the world through gold-tinted glasses. No matter how weird or disturbing a lie is, the optimist more likely than not will not notice it since they are often honest with others and themselves and expect that same honesty back. You can rest assured that it is an optimist who came up with the phrase "benefit of the doubt."

So, are you being targeted by liars? This might not necessarily be the case—yet you should still exercise some caution when dealing with seemingly duplicitous people. People who lie are not necessarily doing so to target anyone in particular. That being said, they will play it by ear, stay flexible, and switch tactics depending on who it is they're interacting with.

In other words, it is possible to be susceptible to the deception in their words, in theory. Also, just because it's easier to lie to certain personalities than others does not mean that everyone else is impervious to being had. A good rule of thumb would be to tread carefully when you are dealing with strangers, at least. This is not advocating that you embrace paranoia; it is simply suggesting that you exercise caution.

Chapter Six: Manipulation Tactics

The Machiavellian can do what they do by manipulating you both psychologically and emotionally. Psychological manipulation happens when the Machiavellian socially influences you to act differently—the way they would prefer. They manipulate to change other people's perceptions and use deceptive, devious, indirect, and immoral tactics. The whole point of manipulation is to get something at the expense of another person. In other words, manipulation is manipulation on account of the exploitation and underhandedness that is going on.

Social influence is not always a bad thing. For instance, if you had a smoking habit, and your doctor, family, and friends did their best to persuade you to quit, that would not necessarily be a bad thing in the end. They have nothing to gain from your quitting. In fact, you are the one who is going to benefit the most from giving in to their persuasion. In this case, you're not being manipulated, merely persuaded. Another key difference between persuasion and manipulation is that the former is fine as long as everyone respects that you do not have to do as you are asked, and you're not under duress or being forced to comply with the suggestions. You and you alone can accept what they're suggesting, or trash it.

Key Aspects of Manipulation

For the manipulator to manipulate, they have to:

1. Hide their evil intentions and act like they are friendly and harmless.

2. Know the various ways in which their target is psychologically vulnerable so that they can figure out the best manipulative tactics to use.

3. Be ruthless enough to have no issues with harming their target when necessary.

Here is how the Machiavellian operates when it comes to maintaining control of the people they manipulate:

1. *They use positive reinforcement.* They will praise you, be all charming—except said charm is really superficial—throw money at you, show fake sympathy, give you approval, apologize more than is needed, give you lavish gifts and attention, force their smiles and laughter, and also publicly recognize you for having done well.

2. *They also use negative reinforcement.* They will offer to get you out of a terrible situation if you agree to do what they want you to do.

3. *They use partial or intermittent reinforcement, both positive and negative.* When it is the former, they can encourage you to keep going with whatever they want you to do. When it's the latter, they have you feeling a lot of doubt and fear about doing what you want to.

4. *They will flat-out punish you.* That punishment will include silent treatment, yelling, nagging, swearing, intimidation tactics, guilt-tripping, crying, emotional blackmail, sulking, and acting like the victim.

5. *They will cause you trauma just one time.* They do this so that you learn to fall in line. They can use explosive anger, verbal abuse, and other forms of intimidation to show you that they're the top dog, and they will take no guff from you or anyone. When you have experienced their reproach once, you're more than likely to find ways not to upset the person doing the manipulating.

Manipulative Techniques

Technique #1: Lying by omission. The Machiavellian chooses to withhold the most vital aspects of the truth.

Technique #2: Lying by the commission. Here, the truth is skewed; however, you cannot tell when the liar is lying to you. Keep in mind that the Machiavellian is a master at deception, and lies often and subtly.

Technique #3: Rationalization. The Machiavellian will come up with some excuse for why they acted as they did, even though it was totally inappropriate.

Technique #4: Denial. They refuse to fess up about what they have done.

Technique #5: Diversion. They do not give you a straightforward answer. They'd rather evade it by changing the topic.

Technique #6: Minimization. This involves both rationalization and denial. The Machiavellian will continue to insist that what they did was not as terrible or dangerous as someone says. They're the ones quick to dismiss cutting remarks they make as "just jokes."

Technique #7: Guilt-tripping. The Machiavellian will tell you, "You don't care at all. You're so selfish! I don't blame you, though. It's only because you've got an easy life." These kinds of statements make you feel guilty, so you find you are always anxious, you doubt yourself all the time, and you're submissive when it comes to them.

Technique #8: Covert intimidation. The manipulator will deliberately get you defensive by making implied, subtle, indirect threats, veiled just enough for you to get the message, and for others to miss it.

Technique #9: Vilification. The Machiavellian is all about getting you defensive with this very powerful technique. Not only are you defensive, but they also do a good job of covering the intent of their message and go one step further: They make you—the actual victim—seem like the abuser when you decide to defend yourself.

Technique #10: Shaming. The Mach will be sarcastic as they put you down in the presence of others. This serves to up the ante when it comes to how much you and everyone else fears them, and it also makes you doubt yourself. The shaming technique is not always so obvious. Sometimes it is only in their tone of voice; other times, it's an angry, intense look. They might make rhetorical comments you cannot respond to with an ever so subtle dash of sarcasm. They can make you feel scared or ashamed for attempting to stand up to them. It's a great way to make their targets feel terrible.

Technique #11: Acting the victim. The Machiavellian is fine with making themselves seem like the long-suffering victim of someone else, or circumstance, just to get people to feel bad for them or reach out to them and strengthen their relationships. The trouble is that the victims often have an actual heart, and their love and care inevitably put an X on their back for the Machiavellian to take aim and fire.

Technique #12: Acting the servant. They will mask their selfish agenda in a way that makes it seem like a noble cause. They'll say things like, "Hey, I'm just doing my job," when in all honesty, they're just taking pleasure from treating you dreadfully or seeing you in pain.

Technique #13: Blaming others. The Mach will seek out scapegoats and in the subtlest of ways, so subtle that you would find it hard to spot it. They will project their thoughts onto you and make it look like you are in the wrong. Even when you catch them in their lies and expose them for who they are, they will still blame you for being gullible in the first place, as though they had no choice but to exploit and deceive you for being so open and trusting. The only time the manipulator is okay with accepting the blame is when they want to seem like they feel remorseful.

Technique #14: Pretending innocence. The Mach will try to make you think they did not mean to hurt you. They'll lie and say that they didn't do what you're accusing them of. They may even feign surprise and act indignant. When they do this, you will start to wonder if you actually experienced things as you did, or if you're losing your mind.

Technique #15: Pretending confusion. The Machiavellian will act stupidly as they have absolutely no clue what you are talking about. They will act like they're confused whenever you address a serious issue with them. They will do all they can to make you confused so that you wonder if your version of events is actually valid, or your sanity is slipping. They will point out certain key points, which they had in place, like contingency plans for just the occasion. They will also have made sure they have people who can back up their story, either innocently or with as much malevolent intent as the Machiavellian itself.

Technique #16: Bandwagon effect. The Machiavellian will make you submit by comforting you, saying that a lot of people have already done whatever you are doing, and so you might as well do it too. They'll say things like, "People just like you . . ." or "Everyone's doing it."

Technique #17: Anger as a weapon. The Machiavellian will use anger like a weapon, brandishing it as intensely as they can to shock you into a submissive state. It seems like they are angry, but they're not. It is all an act. They want what they want from you, and they know that if they act angry, chances are you'll give it to them. They can manipulate you with controlled anger so that they do not have to deal with the embarrassment of a confrontation between you both, or they can hide their real intentions, or they can keep the truth hidden. They'll threaten to call the cops or threaten to make false reports.

Along with controlled anger, you get blackmail. The Machiavellian uses anger to avoid having to tell the truth when they don't want to. They use anger as a shield or defense mechanism so that all suspicions and inquiries are dead on arrival.

Real-World Examples of Manipulation

Meredith was concerned for her close friend Kayla. Kayla had a boyfriend named Jeff, who would always threaten her with suicide each time she tried to break up with him. She had very valid reasons to leave because he was verbally, physically, and sexually abusive. Finally, Meredith convinced Kayla to seek professional help, and in time, Kayla worked up the guts to end things with Jeff. He tried to threaten suicide to get her to stay again, but this time around, Kayla didn't give in. He was finally put on suicide watch, and Kayla made sure to block him from ever contacting her again. Threatening suicide is one thing manipulators do to keep people in line.

Ben had to deal with a manipulator at work who would never stick to the facts and would always accuse him of one thing or the other. One day, Ben had enough.

His boss had summoned him to the office and said, "You're disrespectful!"

Where Ben would ordinarily cower, this time around, he asked her, "How was I disrespectful?"

His boss was speechless, and this only made her livid. "I don't know, and I don't care! All I know is that you're incredibly disrespectful!"

So, Ben tried again by asking, "Who was I disrespectful to? Tell me, and I'll make it right." However, his boss had no concrete answer. It became pretty obvious his boss only wanted to manipulate him and bait him into reacting emotionally, but Ben had foiled her plans.

Ben pressed further by asking, "What have you heard me say or seen me do that makes you feel I'm disrespectful?"

His boss could do nothing but stutter in response. She never bothered him again.

Nigel had a relationship with Anita for two years, and he suffered unspeakable trauma. Anita would always take every chance she could to tell Nigel he did not remember things right, or that he had forgotten how things actually played out. As if this were not enough trouble for Nigel, he had schizoaffective disorder, which meant he had altered states and memory lapses. Nigel eventually figured out what was going on when he started speaking with other people going through the same thing. Once Anita had won an argument with him, she would make Nigel question his sanity and memory. She would swoop in and act like the angel, the good woman who was so forgiving and loving toward her broken boyfriend. She would remind him repeatedly that no matter what anyone had to say about it, she would never judge Nigel for his memory lapses.

Charles's ex-wife Lucy was well aware that he wanted a PS4 when the game console was released. It was all he could talk about. So, when Lucy wanted to do something, and she was well aware Charles would not enjoy at all, she would call him up on the phone while he was at work to let him know there was a surprise waiting for him at home. Days before she made that phone call, she would make subtle hints about the PS4 to Charles, and he would have it in mind. When she did call, she would do so several times to get him really excited by how amazing the surprise is, and how she could not wait for him to have it.

Charles would fall for it each time. He would arrive home, and there she'd be, proudly presenting him with some cheap necklace or a vest that she knew Charles would hate. She would watch him like a hawk, looking for a reaction that said he did not enjoy the gift. Once she realized he was extremely disappointed, she would start in with the crocodile tears.

"You don't like it? I don't believe it! Do you have any idea how much this cost? How long I had to wait to get it? You are incredibly insensitive and so ungrateful! You have no idea just how to hurt I feel right now!"

And on and on, she would go, accusing Charles of not being appreciative of her efforts. Inevitably, Charles would feel guilty, and then he would have to do whatever it was Anita wanted to placate her.

The second Charles gave Anita whatever it was she wanted the most, she would suddenly not care one bit about the "gift" she had gotten him. In fact, he actually wore one of the vests she'd gotten him once, and she had asked him, "Oh my goodness . . . Where did you get that hideous thing?"

Charles says Anita was a compulsive liar and a great manipulator—except when she hit the bottle.

Chapter Seven: Dark Negotiation Tactics

Negotiation is the process of coming to a mutually beneficial agreement. It often involves coming to a compromise or an understanding while making sure to avoid disputes and arguments. For some reason, many people are frightened about negotiating when there is really nothing to it other than striking a bargain—or at least, that is all it should be. The trouble happens when you're negotiating with someone who is Machiavellian or part of the dark triad. In this situation, it's easy to feel intimidated because they're actually experts at getting you to do whatever they want you to do, and unlike other normal people, they're not afraid to use dirty tricks and throw their weight around till you cower and hand over whatever they're asking for.

The Machiavellian and Dark Negotiation

In dark negotiation, there is no consideration for a win-win scenario. Even when it seems that way on the outset, you will find in the end that you have been shortchanged. Ethics or morals do not bind the Machiavellian, and so they are not afraid to play the negotiation game as low and as dirty as possible. So, it would be in your best interest to learn the kinds of tactics they use to coerce you into a position you'd really rather not be in.

Dark Negotiation Tactics

Tactic #1: *Fake disappointment.* The Machiavellian knows how powerful it is to act disappointed. It's not just anecdotal; science also backs this up. Research has shown that when you seem disappointed during negotiations, fewer demands are made of you, and more concessions are made to you. The reason for this is that the other person will feel the need to give you more to put you both on equal footing or make you feel better about the deal you're striking.

The Machiavellian is well aware of the power of acting disappointed. In fact, they will go so far as acting like they do not like the offer you've given them when, in all honesty, they could be ecstatic about what they've gotten out of you so far. The Machiavellian knows two things:

1. If they act unhappy, it's possible for them to be happier than they already are since they can ask for more.

2. If they act happy, it might make you think you should offer even less, or you should think twice about your offer to them.

The best negotiators—and Machiavellians—know never to take the first thing they're offered. They also know this: Never show you're impressed.

Block: When the Machiavellian acts unhappy, let them know that, unfortunately, there's not much else you can offer them, but if they let you know what it is they want, you can pass it along to the head honcho or a higher authority.

Tactic #2: "You're gonna have to do better than that." The pro negotiator or Machiavellian—these are not necessarily the same—knows to use the phrase. Then they stay silent and allow you to come forward and make a concession that works for them.

Block: When you hear that line, you must respond by asking something to the effect of, "Okay. How much better are we talking?" When you answer this, you remain in charge of the negotiation. You also avoid making the mistake of going over and beyond what they really want from you.

Tactic #3: *"Don't be so defensive."* When you hear this one, know that the manipulator is using reverse psychology on you. Often, this line will come up when the Machiavellian is well aware that you are not playing ball with them. If they sense you don't trust them, they'll ask you not to be so defensive, and they might follow that line up with a joke to get you to let your guard down. If you laugh or smile good-naturedly, it means you're going along with them, agreeing that yes, you are being too defensive, and you need to be more willing to make some more concessions.

Block: Do not ever respond by saying you're not defensive. If you do that, you will find yourself psychologically primed into acting more trusting, open, and trustworthy just to prove to them that they are wrong, and this puts the power right in their hands. Instead, you should say something like this: "Your method in dealing with me is making me defensive. If you want to get into that, I'll tell you precisely how and why." Replying this way puts the power squarely in your hands. On the other hand, you can simply reply with a joke like, "Offer me a better deal, and I'll put my sword and shield down." Make sure to smile, but in a way that doesn't reach your eyes. As you do, make sure you hold their gaze. Whatever you do, never look away, and never blink till they concede or change tactics.

Tactic #4: *Create a non-existent higher authority that makes it tough to concede.* How can you tell you are negotiating with an idiot? When they put themselves forward as the last bus stop or final authority. If the person you're negotiating with lets you know they have some "leeway for agreeing on a price," they don't have any power. The powerful negotiator knows to act like their nothing but an errand boy, a lamb, a mouthpiece. They act like they couldn't possibly decide all by themselves, and they'll need to check with the head honchos to figure out whether or not they can make the concessions you seek. With this non-existent leverage, they can play all sorts of games with you. They also have the advantages of:

1. Buying time while they "ask" their "people."

2. Seeming tough without being nasty about it. (They can claim they'd give you what you want, but they've got really tough bosses.)

3. Playing the last-minute agreement or concession trick on you (which will be detailed later in the book).

Block: There are several ways you can deal with this dark negotiation tactic:

1. Act as if you believe them while keeping in mind what game they're playing with you.

2. You can say, "Hey now, are we really playing good cop, bad cop?"

3. You can also say, "Great! When are you going to meet with them? I'd love to be there so I can talk with them too."

4. Or you can say, "Oh come on, you're the boss/expert/head honcho. I bet the others will have to go with your decisions anyway, don't they?"

Tactic #5: *Wrestle a last-minute agreement with fake last-minute snags.* It is not uncommon for the manipulator to wait until the last minute to tell you, "Something just came up." They do this to get a last-minute concession out of you.

At first, everything goes swimmingly well. In fact, they have greenlit the transaction, and they let you know they just need to check in with the boss or the board, and it all sounds like it's a solid, done deal. However, at the last minute, they come back to you to let you know the board or the boss is being difficult, and so you have no choice but to make a concession.

Block: When they let you know that the people in charge are difficult, let them know you will also need to get back to your people, or you are going to have to think over what they're telling you. If you're in a situation where they need you a lot more than you need them, you should go ahead and exploit that. You can say,

"Look, Joe, I thought long and hard about this, and I really would like to hold on to my end of the bargain. But I've had time to crunch the numbers, and every day I'm busier and busier with more demand, and . . . I hate to have to go back on my word, but considering the way the market is, I've got to charge you ten percent more for it to be worth my while. Now, since I gave you a much different price than this, I'm willing to cut that down to five percent, but only for you. So, let me know by the end of the day."

Tactic #6: *Good cop, bad cop.* You already know how this one goes. Here are the different ways this can play out:

1. The bad cop acts strictly while the good cop acts more agreeable.

2. The bad cop acts enraged and storms out of the room, while the good cop acts like a friend.

3. The good cop lets you know they'd give you what you're asking for, but the powers that be—also known as "bad cop"—won't let them.

Block: Have your very own bad cop, real or fake. Alternatively, you can act like you're falling for their ruse, and then use it to your advantage so you can see what it is they offer you. When the person acting as the good cop offers you a deal, they will have shown you their hand. They've automatically let you know what works for them—which is what you must absolutely not accept.

Tactic #7: *Let them come to you.* When it comes to negotiations, the perceived power is very important. The more power you have, the more concessions you get in a negotiation because the weaker negotiator is forced to give you what you want. Here are some subtle ways in which the negotiator can demonstrate power over you:

- Come over to my office (or home, or their preferred location.)

- I am only free from 7 AM to 7:30 AM, is that good for you?

- I am quite busy this week. Let's talk next week, all right?

When you can avoid it, do not go to their home or office, or wherever they want you to meet. If you meet them on their turf, it basically says that they have more power. It also makes them feel much more secure, which means they have the advantage.

Block: Propose your preferred location, or ask them to meet you halfway. Another thing you should never do is chase them too hard—unless you are willing to give your power away, or it is part of your long-term strategy.

Tactic #8: *Encirclement.* This involves being outnumbered. The start of negotiations is often a tug of war, where the game is about holding on to the most power. The way these tactic works is simple—the negotiator shows up with a bunch of other people, and that can make you feel automatically defensive. If you notice that they are all sitting on one side of the table, or worse, all around you, they're basically trying to frame the situation into a "many versus one" situation. In case it is just you and two other people negotiating, be mindful if one of them sits opposite you while the other chooses to sit by your side. They might be springing for the good cop versus bad cop game.

Block: You should say to them, "I expected only Joe. Why are you here with more friends?" The negotiator might reply, "They're actually also interested, and they had time to join us, so now we're here, let's sit down and talk, shall we?" In this case, you should respond, "Rather than try to play negotiation games, let's come up with a win-win solution. Okay?"

If you are unafraid of seeming really bold, and you know for a fact there is absolutely no need for other people to be involved in the negotiation, you can try saying this: "Listen, I've been in contact with you, Joe, and if it's not too much trouble, I'd rather talk with just one person. The more people involved, the more it gets complicated. I'd rather keep it as simple as possible." Then add, while staring at the other uninvited people, "I know a great place in the area I can recommend to you guys where you can grab drinks and great food."

Tactic #9: *Nibbling—or the "last drops" technique.* Say you are done negotiating and so close to signing papers. You can finally relax and maybe even spend time socially with your negotiator for some beer. Now, you let your hair down, and you're excited about wrapping things up. Just as you go out to celebrate, the Machiavellian or pro negotiator will do their best to milk you for some concessions or get the "last drops" of champagne out of you.

They may say, "By the way, you're going to write bonus material for the book, right?" If your response is "no" or that the time is not right to tack on any more clauses to your agreement, they will do their best to make it seem like it was already obvious that you would have to do what they're asking. They might do this by saying, "Oh, come on now. The only reason we didn't talk about it is that's the standard procedure. Everyone's got to agree to write bonuses."

Block: You have to control the frame. You can do this by saying, "No, that isn't right. You claim everyone's got to, but who's everyone? In my experience, no one does, and no one asks for that. So, don't try to mess things up when we've already come to a great arrangement for us both."

Here are other ways you can deal with it:

- Smile like they are just joking.
- Let them know that the deal they already have is pretty awesome as it stands, and that's the end of it.
- Let them know that after that dark move they just pulled, dinner, after the papers are signed, is on them. But, if they are quick enough to get you to sign, you might be nice enough to still celebrate with them. Then offer a sweet smile and wait.

Tactic #10: *Flinch at First Sight.* A great negotiator will be quick to "flinch" when you make your first offer. It is a powerful nonverbal response that says, "Are you nuts? Cut that number way,

way down, right now!" If you come down right away, you are no longer in a position of power and will lose all credibility.

The flinch could be a dramatic shout as they repeat your offer back to you, or it could be as subtle as them taking a step back and sighing. More often than not, a good negotiator will choose not to go the dramatic route, as that is a great way to ruin the rapport and comes off as insulting toward you and the product you're offering.

Rather than get loud, they might pause and seem flustered and thoughtful, almost like they are saying, "I really want this, but that price is too crazy!" Then they might compliment you and try to hype you up as they execute the flinch. It could be something like this: "Well, I get why you want to get paid that much. I mean, it's you. Your work speaks for itself, and I'm a huge fan. I would really love to work out a way to work with you." They're building rapport and buttering you up to make you softer so you can drop your price and not lose face. A terrible negotiator would try to make you or your service seem worthless.

Block: Never go back on your first offer straightaway. If you do, you are done. Instead, you should ask what it is they are thinking, and when they offer you their deal, you should flinch in response too. If they're buttering you up, you can simply reply, "Thank you. I'd really love to work with you, too, so I really hope somehow you can figure out a way to pay the proper and fair price, so we can get started immediately."

There are many games the dark negotiator plays. Keep your eyes wide open.

Chapter Eight: Persuasion Techniques and Principles

Persuasion is all about influencing other people's attitudes, motivations, beliefs, behaviors, and intentions. When it happens in business, it is about changing the attitude of a group or a person toward an object, or an idea, or other people or groups, while making use of visual tools, spoken and written words, and whatever else will help to pass along feelings, reasonings, and information in general. It's also about making use of your resources, both personal and positional, to have people thinking or behaving the way you would like them to.

You can either opt for systematic persuasion, where you change attitudes and behaviors by appealing to reason and logic or go for heuristic persuasion, where you appeal to people's emotions or habits to get them to swing your way.

The 21 Principles of Persuasion

You have probably wondered how it is that some people are incredibly persuasive. How do they get so skilled at getting others to see things their way? Well, the following 21 principles will help you learn to be persuasive and spot when a Machiavellian is in the process of persuading you so that you can keep your guard up.

#1: *Persuasion and manipulation are two different things.* Manipulation involves being coerced to do something that is definitely not in your best interests. On the flip side, persuasion is about getting people to do things that will benefit them in the long run—and benefit you.

#2: *Only ever try to persuade those who can be persuaded.* Sure, you can persuade everyone, but only when the timing and the context are right. However, just because everyone can be persuaded does not mean that they can be persuaded right away. Many political campaigns spend a lot of their money and time on just a small group of swing voters who usually determine the winner of an election. There is a reason for that. So, the first thing you want to do is figure out who, at a certain time, can be persuaded to see things your way. Then, give them all of your attention and energy.

#3: *The timing and context matter.* These two things are fundamental to the art of persuasion. It is the context that gives a baseline for what is okay. The timing is what sets the tone for what you want from other people and life. You would rather marry someone different from the sort of person you dated in your younger years because your wants and needs naturally change over time. Just because the person you want to persuade wanted something yesterday doesn't mean they are still desperate to have it today.

#4: *Only those who are interested can be persuaded.* You cannot persuade someone who does not care about what you are offering them. For the most part, no one cares about you. They only care about number one—themselves. Everyone's thoughts are preoccupied with health, money, or love. To persuade people, you need to understand how to talk to them about themselves. If you learn to keep the spotlight on them, they will keep their eyes and ears focused on you.

#5: Reciprocity is a compelling force. For some reason, when someone does something for you, you feel the need to do something for them. It is hardwired in people's brains that they should help others to thrive. You—or the Machiavellian—can use this need to reciprocate to persuade other people. When you offer small, meaningful gestures to others, you automatically can ask for a lot more from them in return—and they'll be happy to help you.

#6: Be persistent. It pays. Whoever is able and willing to continue to ask for the things they want, and continues to offer value consistently, is often the most persuasive person. For this reason, many historical leaders have been able to rally the masses to be on their side.

#7: Be sincere in your compliments. Everyone loves sincere compliments. Something about them puts a pep in one's step. People tend to trust those who make them feel good. So, putting two and two together, it becomes obvious that when you can, you should compliment other people. Be sincere, and even better, compliment things about them that they are not usually praised for. When you offer sincere compliments, it is much easier to persuade other people.

#8: Set concrete expectations. A huge part of persuasion is effectively managing other people's expectations so they can trust your choices. Say you are a CEO, and you promise to rake in twenty percent more in sales, but you pull in thirty percent more— you will definitely be rewarded. However, if you promise 40 percent, but you pull in only 37, you're sure to get punished. In other words, make sure you underpromise and overdeliver.

#9: Never assume. Do not think you know what it is the next person needs. Just make your value plain. Unfortunately, especially in the world of sales, many people will not bother to offer their service or products because they make the erroneous assumption that others don't have any interest or don't have the money to pay. Never assume what people want. Just make your offer and let them decide.

#10: *Manufacture scarcity.* The value of everything is relative. People tend to want things because other people want these things. When you want someone to want what you have, you must make that thing scarce—even when you are the object of desire.

#11: *Manufacture urgency.* You must make the people you are persuading feel like they need to make a decision and act immediately. If they are not driven enough to want something from you right away, chances are they won't be driven in the future either. You must persuade the people in the here and now, and you can do this by playing up the urgency or inducing FOMO—the fear of missing out.

#12: *Pictures are potent.* More potent than what you hear is what you see. That is the reason you watch a commercial for a drug, where the setting is a happy place with smiling people, while in a low tone and superfast, there's a voice-over talking about the drug's deadly side effects. Pictures say a lot more than words. So, you must be willing to give a great first impression in the minds of the people you're persuading.

#13: *Tell the truth.* If you want to persuade someone, you should tell them stuff about themselves that no one else will say. There is nothing more meaningful than being confronted with the hard truth about you. When you tell people the truth, with no agenda and no judgment, not only will people respect you more, but they'll also be more open to being persuaded.

#14: *Establish rapport.* For some reason, people like others who are similar to themselves. This affects every decision they make, consciously and subconsciously. When you mirror and match other people's behaviors, including patterns of speech, body language, speech cadence, and so on, it is easy to create rapport with others so that they are more comfortable being around you, and therefore more open to your suggestions.

#15: *Be flexible in your behavior.* Often, the person who has control over the situation or interaction is the one who is the most flexible, not the person who's wielding the most power. Many children are extremely persuasive because they are willing to run through the whole gamut of all the behaviors they need to get what they want. They will be charming, pout, bargain, cry, plead—whatever they have to do. While as a parent, all you can do is say "no." You should have a collection of behaviors you can resort to. That way, you will be much more persuasive.

#16: *Become a master of energy transference.* There are people whom you spend time with who leave you completely drained. In contrast, others pump you full of energy. The people who are the most persuasive are masters at infusing others with energy. They transfer their energy to others to fire them up and get them feeling motivated. They do this using physical touch, eye contact, laughter, excitement in their speech, or just listening actively.

#17: *Be clear in your communication.* You must explain your ideas and point of view so that even a kid could get it. If you can't, it is way too complicated. If you are going to be persuasive, you have to keep things as simple as possible and make sure to communicate the core meaning of whatever idea you're trying to pass along.

#18: *Preparation puts you way ahead.* You must make sure that you are well aware of whom you're dealing with and the circumstances. When you do your best to be ready, you will effectively persuade others. For instance, if you learn everything you can about a prospective employer and their services, products, and background, chances are you will be more than prepared for an interview, and you will most likely land the gig.

#19: *Be detached and calm in conflict.* When tempers are flying all around you, it helps to keep a level head. When you are the one who remains on tilt, you will also be the one in control. You must learn to keep your cool, remain calm and detached, and forget your emotions for the time being. When there is conflict, it is to you that people will turn to. It is you that people will trust, and you will be right there to lead them where they need to go.

#20: *Be deliberate in your anger.* It is a rare person who is at peace with conflict. If you want to increase the level of conflict and tension in a situation, most others want the opposite and would rather back down. You can use this to your advantage but do so sparingly. Whatever you do, don't do it out of a lack of self-control or from an emotional position. Just keep in mind that you can use anger as a tool to get people to go along with your vision.

#21: *Be certain and confident.* There is nothing quite as attractive as being confident in who you are and your decisions. When you are sure of yourself, other people find it intoxicating and compelling. They will be more than willing to do as you ask. If you truly buy into what you do, it will take little to nothing to get others to do what would serve them while you get what you want from them as well.

Persuasion vs. Manipulation

Every day, people persuade other people. Each time, it is because they have a vested interest in getting them to do what they would like them to do. There is nothing wrong with persuasion; it's a natural part of human interaction. You can think of it from an altruistic point of view, as you'd like to see a better world, and so you persuade people to act better or hold better beliefs that would foster that sort of world.

It could be that you are just trying to make some money. There is nothing immoral with making money. That said, the people you're trying to persuade to buy from you are looking for reasons to hold on to their money. You have to let them know why they should agree to part with their money and what is in it for them if they hand it over.

Manipulation is using deceitful, unfair, and artful methods to influence others to serve your selfish goals. The thing about manipulation is that it never leads to a win-win scenario. The manipulator is only out for themselves. This is the key difference between persuasion and manipulation. The former seeks mutual benefit or the benefit of others; the latter seeks selfish gain.

If you ever find yourself wondering what you are doing—persuading someone or manipulating them—you only need to ask yourself, "What's in it for the other person?" If you cannot honestly come up with something that benefits them, but you have no problems coming up with all the ways influencing them would benefit you, you are being manipulative.

Manipulation might work in the interim, but it always leaves a wake of dissatisfaction. People sooner or later get sick of the Machiavellian's antics, and their outcry and rage become too intense to sweep under the rug. So, in the end, it is much better to persuade people. It's better to let them have their own reasons for joining your cause, as these reasons are genuine, and the people are intrinsically motivated. The trouble with extrinsic motivation is that it's pretty easy to drop—especially when they realize you are a manipulator who never actually follows through with their promises. Unlike you, a Machiavellian has no noble intentions. They do not merely persuade; they manipulate. You never have to worry about whether or not you are doing right by other people, as long as you make a point of seeking out scenarios where everybody wins and is happy. Seek the greater good for all involved, and paradoxically you will garner all the support you need—from everyone who knows you—to achieve your lofty ideals.

Chapter Nine: Non-Verbal Deception

To talk about nonverbal deception, you must get into nonverbal communication. There are other ways people communicate with each other besides actually speaking, and these methods altogether make up nonverbal communication. Nonverbal communication is just as important as the stuff people say, as it lends much more context and richness of meaning to whatever they are saying or hearing. The trouble is, in this day and age, people are so used to doing a lot of business over the phone or using emails so much that a good number of people are starting to lose touch with the nuances that are a part of face-to-face conversations. It is important to check this because, in the end, nothing beats a live connection with other people.

Albert Mehrabian, a psychologist and also the author of the bestselling book *Silent Messages: Implicit Communication of Emotions and Attitudes,* has conducted research on the matter of nonverbal communication and discovered that with all messages, only about seven percent of meaning is passed on through words, while the remaining 93 percent is passed on through silent, nonverbal communication—and more often than not, the nonverbal communication says much more than words ever could.

Ways People Communicate Nonverbally

Facial expression: This is very common and revealing. Look in a mirror. The face staring back at you can make over 10,000 various expressions, with each one giving tones of meaning and info easily. Frowning, smiling, blinking, and rolling your eyes are expressions that are relatable and strong. Flaring your nostrils or twitching your eyebrows are expressions that also convey meaning with no effort. If you want to connect with someone you do not know, all you have to do is smile at them! When you do, you are welcoming them, setting a warm frame, and making it so that the other person wants to spend time with you.

Body movement (also called kinesics): Body movement includes hand gestures and nodding. With your body, you can let people know you are excited about something. Think of the woman or man who loves to gesture wildly with their hands. There are other aspects of kinesics, too, like the stuff people would associate with anxiety—clearing your throat, trembling, or shaking your leg. When you're in a meeting, you want to make sure your hands are on the table or gently clasped together. Don't keep touching your face, or drumming on the table or your thigh, because these things are not only distracting but can communicate that you're not paying attention.

Posture: Posture is how you hold your body, which often makes a strong and lasting impression on people. The way you sit or stand is critical when it comes to how people perceive you. If you stand with your back straight and your head held high, it says you are strong, confident, and screams assurance in volumes. If you slouch or look to the ground, it says you're weak, uncertain, and perhaps indifferent. If you want to show people that you're friendly, keep your posture open. You want to stand with both legs hip-width

179

apart, keeping your torso open rather than covering it by crossing your arms. Your head should be held high, and your face should be relaxed. When you cross your arms in a closed posture, you're telling people you do not want to be approached, or, at best, bored, and at worst, hostile.

Eye contact: You would be hard-pressed to find a better way to establish rapport with strangers than by holding eye contact. When you maintain eye contact, it means you are paying attention. You're interested and involved. If you do not hold eye contact, it could be read as you being rude, disinterested, or distracted. Holding eye contact does not mean you should stare right into their face—that is actually an intimidation tactic. You want to look sort of randomly around their eyes, including the eyebrows and eyelids.

Paralanguage: This involves the parts of verbal communication that have nothing to do with words and affect the meaning of the words being said. If you have ever had to tell a petulant teen, "Don't take that tone with me," you know exactly what this refers to—things like sarcasm, where the tone of their voice does not match what they're saying. For instance, someone saying "How thrilling" in a less than thrilling tone of voice is clearly not thrilled—and you got that from their tone, not the words themselves. Or if someone makes a presentation and the whole time they just mumble as quickly as they can, it could let you know that they're disingenuous or just nervous. On that note, be aware of how fast you talk. Make sure you speak up and clearly so that everyone can hear you. This doesn't mean you should get too loud, though, because not only does it seem belligerent and uncouth, it's also off-putting.

Proxemics: Proxemics is all about how close or far away someone is when you talk to them. You may have heard the term "close talker." For the most part, people are very aware and protective of their private, personal space—also called the "intimate space" by Mehrabian. This space is typically about six to eight inches. This zone is only ever for close friends, family, and romantic partners. When you are talking business at work, often you will be much further than that from the other people—just far away enough that everyone's comfortable, but not too far to seem uninterested or like you're deliberately distancing yourself.

Physiological changes: Emotions are closely linked to nonverbal communication. You will find that you have the most physiological responses when you're feeling uncomfortable or anxious. Blushing, flushing, sweating, itchy armpits, and tears in your eyes make it obvious that you're not feeling so great right now. When you notice that someone you're talking to is not feeling okay or is nervous, you should do what you can to make them feel at ease. You can often tell from the pitch of their voice and the clamminess of their palms when you shake them whether or not they're nervous.

Nonverbal Deception

Because the Machiavellian is well aware that their body language can give them away, they are careful to act in congruent ways with the lies that they're spinning you. The way the body responds to big lies is often dependent on the liar's fear that they will be discovered or something will give them away, and they will have to deal with major consequences. Research has shown that the expectations surrounding how a liar acts when they're lying are wrong—whether those expectations are of the layperson or professional interrogators. You cannot just see someone sweating bullets and assume they're telling a lie. Maybe it is hot, or they really need to go to the bathroom.

When some people lie, they look you in the eye. Others do not. Some will look frozen, and others will move about like a motivational speaker. They might look one way when they are trying to put one over you and look the same way when they're not. They can deliberately set up their nonverbal cues to seem like they're honest.

The fact is you may be able to see nonverbal behavior, but you can only guess what each behavior means or what is causing it. Just because someone is nervous during an interview does not mean that the interview is the problem. It also does not mean they're lying—perhaps it's their first interview. The way to take a look at nonverbal behavior and deception is to look at the behavior more as an alert or a cause for concern, or a clue that you might want to ask more questions to gauge the actual cause of the problem.

Nonverbal Deception Cues

While you cannot and should not make assumptions about whether someone is lying based on these cues alone, you should know what to look out for to press the issue at hand further and get to the truth.

Gestures can let you know when you are being lied to. Studies show that liars will often gaze downwards and move their heads and hands in a faster or slower way than usual. Again, you should never use nonverbal cues to detect deception. What you want to do is use them to detect stress, which can help you ask the right questions of the person in question.

Anti-gravity signals are something the liar will also give. According to Joe Navarro, an FBI special agent, the liar will often use gestures that defy gravity, like lifting themselves onto their toes when they are standing, often at the end of their sentence, to make their point clearer. Or they raise their toes when they're seated. Another thing they do is raise their eyebrows, which means they trust the words they are spinning.

The palm-up gesture often gives a clue about deception. It shows inability or helplessness. The hand shrug gesture also shows up as a sort of nonverbal slip, letting you know they may not be as honest as they seem.

There is also the self-touch, where the suspected liar will put their hand to their face subconsciously to cover their shame over being deceitful. They might do this by covering their eyes or touching their forehead, all while gazing downward.

When it comes to nonverbal deception, certain changes happen in six categories regarding behavior:

1. Changes that show underlying anxiety.

2. Changes that show withdrawal.

3. Excessive attitudes and displays that do not match with the liar's usual response when they are honest.

4. Changes that show there is a covert negative affect.

5. Changes that show uncertainty and vagueness.

6. Changes that show mixed messages or incongruous responses.

The Power of Nonverbal Cues

Nonverbal cues are much more powerful than words or actions. Within just moments of meeting someone, they will have formed their impression of you, even if they really have no idea who you are. They'll have taken into account your dressing, comportment, and how your body talks. It is just the way human interaction goes.

If you want to make sure that you are hardly ever the victim of deceit, you need to become a human nonverbal communication scholar. The reason is simple: Your body and gestures will often give away a lot more than your words. The same is true for a Machiavellian, and knowing this can help you stay one step ahead of the game.

Nonverbal communication is a great way for you to spot the lack of congruence between what someone tells you and what they really think or feel. The ability to read people skillfully will also keep you from embarrassing situations and losses. Whenever something does not quite feel right, it is often hard for most people to hide that from others, especially if they are close to you. When they do try, what happens more often than not is inevitable conflict and misunderstanding. Nonverbal communication is vital because it is often done unconsciously, meaning it's out of the deceiver's control. So, nonverbal cues are a great way to ascertain an issue not being handled or disclosed as fully as it should be.

Nonverbal cues are also important in therapy as they can provide the therapist with insight into their patients. If the therapist or counselor is well aware of their patient's nonverbal cues and can weigh them against the words they say, they can decide whether or not there is a match between them. It is safe to say that the therapist, more often than not, will learn a lot more from what is not said than from what is being said, and armed with this info, they will find the deeper issues that plague their patients—who may not even be aware of them.

In fact, there is somatic experiencing, which is a kind of therapy that is especially helpful in treating people who deal with trauma. It considers the physical responses and body language of the person undergoing treatment as the counselor or therapist introduces them to the cause of their trauma in small, safe doses. The therapist then deciphers the nonverbal cues to assess where their patient is at regarding recovery.

Nonverbal cues are further significant in body-mind psychotherapy, where the patient's sounds, breaths, and body movements are measured. This is so the therapist can easily pinpoint the patient's behaviors that are counterproductive and then help them develop new, better habits to replace the old behaviors. If you want to get better at reading nonverbal cues, you must observe people around you. Compare and contrast their reactions and behaviors when they speak with you at certain times about specific issues versus other times and other issues. With your eyes open, you will see what is really going on.

Chapter Ten: Who Uses These Tactics?

Manipulation or Deception?

Say you are a salesperson. You are tasked with one job: Getting the prospect to exchange their money for what you're selling. That is a tough thing to do since people are always looking for good reasons not to buy. To get rid of the natural desire to say "no," you would have to resort to certain tactics as a marketer or salesperson.

- You might put up a sign that says, "50% off!"
- Or "2-day sale!"
- Or "Only 7 more left!"

When you use signs like this, your prospect goes from arguing against buying it to thinking it is such a great deal that they would have to be stupid to let it go. These tactics of urgency, scarcity, and exclusivity work very well as you tap into the buyer's lizard brain and get them actually to do something about it. These tactics are persuasion levers, and many people get uncomfortable at the thought of using them because they consider them manipulative. They have a point; it is manipulative. Getting people to swipe their cards is calculating, but it is definitely not the same as deception. So, if you work in sales, or you have ever found yourself in a situation where you had to use these tactics, and you feel gross about it, it's probably because you are assuming manipulation and deception are the same things.

Manipulation is great when you want people to take action. It is using skillful persuasion to get someone to take action concerning their interests. Again, you can only persuade people who are interested in what you are offering—and since everyone only cares about themselves, they're probably interested because they know what you're offering could be good for them. All you're doing is letting them know why they should not just get it but get it right now.

This being said, some salespeople do not care about making claims that are unsubstantiated if it means it will bring them sales.

People Who Use Deceptive Tactics

There are certain industries where liars thrive. Salespeople have already been discussed, so who else is suspect when it comes to deception?

Congress members are not considered the most honest people on account of their wheeling and dealing. There is no surprise that this is the general perception of people in politics as a whole.

Lobbyists, for obvious reasons, are not very honest. You can expect a fair number of them to have Machiavellian traits—if they are not outright Machiavellians—since they need to do what they must to get people to swing their way.

Car salespeople are not generally trusted because people often tend to get the short end of the stick when dealing with them. In fact, according to a Gallup poll, only seven percent of Americans think that car salespeople can be trusted.

Telemarketers do not have a lot of fans. At best, people consider them a nuisance; at worst, they have a propensity to conflate figures, tell tales, and say whatever they need to in order to make you give up your credit card details.

Stockbrokers have a long way to go before they can be considered honest, particularly as the industry is often rife with unethical practices like insider trading and things of that nature. It is a pretty cutthroat industry that often only attracts people who can handle a great amount of pressure.

Business executives are not entirely trusted. There are too many tales of CEOs who are undeniably brilliant but resort to the most underhanded tactics to get their staff to fall in line, improve their bottom line, and take out the competition.

Labor union leaders are not particularly anyone's favorite, because again, there is a lot of manipulation and deals that need to be made, and the temptation to cut corners or do something other than was promised remains very high.

Lawyers can often stray easily into being deceptive. Whether it is altruistic—as in wanting to help their innocent clients—or more from a personal need to win, many cases have lawyers crossing lines that they should not to get their wins.

Real estate agents are pretty suspect sometimes, presenting a pretty picture only for the brand-new homeowner to learn many terrible things after purchasing or paying the lease.

This does not imply that everyone in the industries mentioned above is a deceiver or a Machiavellian, or anything like that. It just means that these professions would work well for a liar and most likely would have a significant number of people for whom lying is as natural as breathing.

Politics and Manipulation

Now you will look at tactics that politicians use to get people to vote for them and support their policies even when it actually would not serve anyone besides themselves.

Appealing to their national pride: One of the ways politicians can get people on their side is by appealing to their national pride. A politician's power is dependent on their ability to get the people to willingly accept their legitimacy, authority, and right to get them to pay taxes. Plus, if a politician can continue to get people to back up the government and the country just because they all belong on the same piece of land and recognize a certain flag as theirs, they can continue to grow in power and influence.

The trouble is that it is not rational to selflessly support a group as far as the average voter is concerned. For this reason, the politician will speak about lofty ideals, worthy causes, and higher values. They will speak of "the great red, white and blue" and serving the country. It's not a coincidence that politicians focus on such ephemeral and vague ideals.

While a persuasive tactic would be getting people to see "What's in it for me," this doesn't play out well in politics since what works even better than social exchange is an appeal to identity. Think about it: If the populace were to think long and hard about what is in it for them if they vote someone in or back them up, they would realize the answer to that question is "Nothing."

Sculpting their voters: Another thing politicians do is carefully sculpt their voters. As Robert Cialdini once wrote, "We like people who are like us," and as such, it is important to the politician to seem like they represent the citizens in many ways. In other words, the politician has to seem like the prototype of the people. Think of George Bush, with his Bushisms, errors in speech, seeming disdain for the bigwigs in DC, and love for steak and beer. He came off looking like the average voter, and that was a genius move on his part, whether or not people got any good out of his administration. You could argue that Bush was the perfect Machiavellian in that he presented his weakness as his most representative quality—which automatically meant he could not possibly be attacked for it. Even when enemies would attack this seeming weakness, all it did was make him stronger.

Creating a sense of community: Politicians also know the importance of creating a community, a bunch of "us," with no "I" in existence. This is how they can get the populace to stop thinking about themselves and think more about the government's interests. The goal is to get people to be less selfish and more focused on the "collective"—except the collective is the politician and their ideals.

Throwing the masses a bone: The higher up you rise in politics, the more you risk losing touch with the grassroots. However, it is also true that the higher you rise, the more leverage you will get when you make yourself accessible to the electorate. The reason for this is simple: If you, as powerful as you are, can come down to their level and be accessible, that will make the public look at you as someone who is very magnanimous. In other words, the best politicians know how important it is to throw the masses a bone.

To understand this phenomenon, just know that the voters would rather have a leader just like them and close to them. If a leader seems too detached or too high up like a king, their followers more likely than not will not willingly put themselves on the line for them or their causes. A politician knows the importance of seeming like they are not just in it for the people; they're in it right beside them. Seeming like they're great friends with the average Joe naturally endears them to everyone.

Creating their enemies: The Machiavellian knows not to make enemies. Instead, they create foes. They can use the enemy like a pawn for their internal power struggles. They work with the mindset that the enemy of their enemy is their friend.

They can also get into an untouchable friendship with a much stronger enemy, allowing for oppression to continue endlessly, like how China defends North Korean dictators. A politician also knows that when they have an enemy, they can use them to generate massive support and trample down all opposition.

The reason this works is brilliant and yet simple. As humans, people have evolved to put aside their differences and come together when faced with mutual enemies. This unity is formed with the politician right at the core of everyone's power, of course. This is why you would be hard-pressed to find a good politician who does not have enemies.

Being unfair to the outliers: The politician is not fair. It is what it is. Even great leaders are never fair. Sure, they will be fair to those who support them, but they will definitely not bother with being fair to those who do not, and this is how they continue to strengthen their leadership.

Every politician understands that the constituency they represent will expect some favorable policies. Everyone knows this is often the case. Even referees judge much more leniently when their home team commits the offense. Some politicians will go as far as pandering only to the interests of their ingroups, to the point where others begin to suffer so that they can get more support from those groups.

Embodying the country: The politician who is smart and persuasive will convince voters that they and they alone are the embodiment of the nation and all its values. When a politician presented themselves this way, automatically they move from being just flesh and blood to become an actual mirror image of the nation, one that is "selfless." When people begin putting up pictures of politicians in their home, that is a sure sign that those politicians have succeeded.

For a moment, think back to Ronald Reagan and his administration, where he was presented as the embodiment of all things American. The Assistant White House Chief of Staff at the time, Richard G. Darman, actually wrote this at the start of Ron's campaign: "Paint RR as the personification of all that is right with or heroized by America. Leave Mondale in a position where an attack on Reagan is tantamount to an attack on America's idealized image of itself—where a vote against Reagan is in some subliminal sense, a vote against mythic 'AMERICA.'"

Reagan did wind up becoming the living embodiment of the values of capitalism and freedom, and so did America, and this started a cycle that powered itself by itself. Of course, it also helped that Reagan was a natural enemy of the USSR. As far as the American public was concerned, it was not the president of the

USA taking on the president of the USSR. For them, it was the living embodiment of capitalism and freedom taking on the communists. In other words, it was much bigger in the minds of the American public than what it really was, and this further cemented the idea that Reagan was a man of the people, by the people, for the people.

The "Great Leader" scam: When the people call on a politician rather than the politician having to push themselves onto the people, they have the best situation ever. It is awesome for them when the people believe that they and they alone can get the job done, whatever it is. In fact, here is the perfect cocktail to political power: Have an enemy, a war to wage, and be the perfect picture of a resolute, tough leader who will take no guff. It would be hard to keep people from voting for such a leader in droves.

This works because crowds will often go to the leader with the most charisma so that they can submit their will to them. This is especially the case when the country is going through a tough time with crisis after crisis. So, for this reason, the dominant leader will continue to promote models of leadership that are individualistic by saying or implying things like how the country needs strong leaders—like themselves. They will also sway the electorate about the troubles and uncertainties in the land—"Let the people state their choice!"

Pretending to be uninterested in power: If a politician looks like they are not interested in power and are in it for the people, they will get all the support they need. So, the politician will go on and on about how they are committed to making beneficial changes for their constituencies without mentioning their actual motives.

People prefer leaders who ignore the benefits of being leaders than those who are only in it for themselves. The politician knows they have to be proponents of major causes like reforms. They will talk about the need for change or to fight this enemy or another. Inevitably, this garners support from the grassroots.

Now take a look at Roosevelt, the one president who ran for a third mandate, and then a fourth. That said, by the end of his second one, things did not seem so clear. If he were definite about what he intended to do, he would have had to deal with a lot of trouble and been accused of being an autocrat.

Roosevelt said he wanted a third mandate. However, he never flat-out said he did not, either, as that would have made it difficult for him to change his mind. Instead, he worked in the background so that all of the other candidates who mattered would not look particularly strong. Roosevelt was a skilled politician and manipulator. He molded himself into the "great leader" by making it clear there was no other or better candidate who could do the job of leading America. With the ongoing war, he deliberately used outside enemies as leverage. Additionally, he acted like he was only serving out of a sense of duty and not because he wanted power.

This section is not meant to bash politics. It is just saying that this field is very attractive to power-hungry people. It's attractive to people like Machiavellians. In the end, they are all just people, for the most part. Do not misconstrue this as some argument for why people should do away with politics altogether. Without it, societies would probably be worse off.

The point here is to help you see how manipulative, persuasive, and deceptive tactics are used in politics. When you know how the game works, you can take an active, more informed role in the governance of your nation as well. Politics should never be up to politicians alone. Everyone is in this together. Thus, you should know how it all works for gaming the system for the greater good or telling when a politician is hoodwinking the entire nation.

Chapter Eleven: Learning to Spot Deception

Body language matters in life. If you notice that the body language and words of the person you are dealing with do not quite match up, there is trouble. Sure, some clues indicate the possibility that someone's telling an outright lie, or they are keeping the truth hidden from you.

When it comes to communication, a lot goes on beyond just speaking, listening, and understanding. Some lies are told only as a matter of courtesy. Say someone asks you how you are. You probably would not want to dump on them about how your lover left you, and your left hip hurts terribly for some reason. You wouldn't get in trouble for telling these lies. Just realize that these are lies that people tend to tell every day.

Lying is incredibly common and sometimes expected. There are even legal strategies that allow for "plausible deniability." So, it is helpful to know how to spot deception so that when you're in a situation where anything less than the truth wouldn't do, you can make sure to get to the bottom of the matter.

The Right and Wrong Ways to Spot Deception

Focusing on eye movement or body language alone is not enough. Many studies have shown that trying to read a lie using body language or eye movement is not effective—even for professional interrogators and law enforcement.

The research on deception has been disappointing for the most part. A lot of it involved trying to gauge the liar's intent by looking at their body language or facial expressions like darting eyes, blushing cheeks, and nervous laughter. Think back to Bill Clinton when he touched his nose as he claimed not to have had an affair with Monica Lewinsky. Everyone assumed that meant he was lying. The thing about lying is that it often generates really intense feelings of guilt, nerves, and sometimes excitement at the prospect of getting away with it. These emotions are difficult to keep in check, so even when you think you have a poker face on, you still have a few "tells" that give you away. These tells are called micro expressions.

The trouble is that the more psychologists dive into the matter, the more they find it difficult to grasp any clues that are reliable enough to let you know when someone is lying. The thing about human behavior is that there is so much variety to it. With enough time, and after becoming very familiar with someone, you might be able to tell what their tics are when they are honest versus when they're shady. However, you cannot apply what you learn about how they act in both situations to other people, as it differs from person to person. In other words, body language has no dictionary that you can reliably turn to when you're confused about what someone's body is saying. There are no signs that always come up when it comes to deception. For some folks, they giggle when they lie. Others get much more serious. Some make heavy eye contact, and some avoid it altogether. There is just no cue you can turn to and say, "Aha! There's the sign that they're lying to me." Even the theory that the subconscious mind can tell when someone is lying or picking up on these cues has been proven untrue.

Despite this, you must still learn when you're being had, and it almost seems like all you have are these cues, almost as mythical as a unicorn. So, you need a way to figure out how to find out when you're being deceived. What do you do? Focus on the liar's words. It's better to ignore all of the subtle cues and mannerisms that people give off when they're lying and instead focus on gently teasing the truth out of them by asking questions until their story starts to crumble. Here is what you need to do:

1. *Make use of open questions.* When you ask open questions, this forces the deceiver to expand their story until they are completely trapped in their lies.

2. *Use the element of surprise to your advantage.* If you want to know if someone is lying, you have to give them much more work. This means asking them questions they do not expect or that are a bit confusing. You can also ask for their version of events, but backward.

3. *Look out for small details that you can verify.* Say someone tells you they study at Harvard—ask them what it is like going there each day. If you notice they said something that is not true, don't let on that you are on to them. Allow them to grow in confidence, and watch as they prattle on with more lies.

4. *Notice how their confidence changes.* Pay attention to the liar and see how their manner of speech changes whenever you decide to challenge them. They might be really talkative when they feel like they are the one in control of the conversation, but if they feel they're losing control, they might decide to clam up and say no more or speak in monotones.

You want to have a casual conversation with them. Do not go "all interrogator" on them. Keep the pressure gentle, and this will be more than enough for the lair to eventually slip up and show their hand by either saying something that doesn't align with the story they have said so far or by getting evasive or responding erratically.

Recall that there is no such thing as a magic bullet when it comes to catching liars. It's about taking all the things that actually work and using them to get results.

Information Trumps a Confession

This is something that is always used in Britain. On account of a ton of false confessions during the mid-80s, the British courts made it official that law enforcement was no longer allowed to use force or aggression to get information out of their suspects. The interrogations are also taped to make sure the officers comply with the new interrogation method, which involves having a chat with the prisoner and beginning with asking questions that the interrogator already knows the answer to. This has helped to reduce the number of false confessions dramatically.

Cheryl Hiscock-Anisman,a forensic psychologist, working at the National University in La Jolla, California, and Kevin Colwell, a forensic scientist, working in Southern Connecticut State University, New Haven, have spent years researching interrogation. They have both realized that those who cook up a story would often cook up an easy to recall script that would be difficult to poke holes in. Those who are honest don't have to use a script since it really did happen as they say it did, and they were there. So, the honest ones will make mistakes, and not only that, they will bring in detail that is unrelated to support their case.

Both Hiscock-Anisman and Colwell have been hard at work to make the contrast between deceivers and honest people much more obvious. Taking what they have learned into the field, they've spent time training officers to look out for patterns in speech misteach of body language and cues. While the San Diego Police Department was, at first, skeptical about their methods, they've since added this method to their toolbox of interrogation methods.

Another thing that helps decide who is lying is to ask the simplest questions. So, the interviewer only has to focus on the words and verbal cues of the person speaking and not the nonverbal stuff. The researchers say it's best to start with a nonthreatening question. For instance, you can ask them what their day was like. They are not likely to lie to you about that—unless they just murdered someone that day and hid the body. The answer will also involve a vivid memory. Coupled with an honest answer, that should give you a baseline for what they are like when they're honest. You know how much information and detail they typically provide when talking about true things.

After establishing a baseline of honesty with the person being interviewed, you can then ask them to let you know about the actual issue at hand or being investigated. When they are done recounting the events, you have to take a step back and compare their responses to both stories. Have you noticed that they use the same number of descriptive phrases? Was there any recall, and was it the same as the first time around? Keep these things in mind as they help you know whether or not you are being lied to.

After this, you must ask a harder question, one which will often give away who is lying and who's being honest. You can say, "Okay, can you go back to when this all happened and walk me through everything again, but do it backward, okay?" What happens all the time is that the liar will have a lot of trouble answering that one. This is a nifty little trick to have for the next time your teenager lies about what they were doing out so late.

Science has shown that when someone is telling the truth, they will give you many little facts. They will give you anecdotal details because they lived the situation as they say they did. In fact, honest people have been proven to give thirty percent more detail than liars.

Truths About Lies

First of all, the perfect liar does not exist. While lying happens every day, it is not something that comes naturally to most people. Often there will be some emotional tell or something that can and will give them away. Another thing is that most people suck at figuring out deception. In other words, as terrible as most people are at lying, they are just as bad at detecting lies.

Now, you cannot go off of blinking alone, but lying can affect how much a liar blinks. A 2008 research article by Stephen Porter and Leanne Brinke of the Forensic Psychology lab at Dalhousie University showed that people who kept their emotions hidden would blink at a much different rate. If they were masking their emotions, they would blink faster. If they were neutralizing the emotions, they would blink a lot slower.

You should also know that it is much harder to fake negative feelings than positive ones. This same article from 2008 showed that it's harder to act sad, fearful, or disgusted than to act happy. According to Universiry of Buffalo's Dr. Mark Frank in a 2013 **PopSci article**, it's harder to fake negative emotions because when you're not feeling great, while one part of the brain works to make you feel how you feel, another works to keep the expression in check. Typically, you wouldn't have this tug of war going on when you're feeling happy.

Liars will often use many different words than those who tell the truth. In that 2012 study, it was demonstrated that they would use many more tentative words and speak a lot less.

An interesting thing about lies is that it is hard to lie to someone if you are attracted to them. Another study carried out in 1985 by DePaulo, Stone, and Lassiter, titled *Telling Ingratiating Lies: Effects of Target Sex and Target Attractiveness on verbal and nonverbal deceptive success,* focused on white lies that people tell to make sure everyone gets along. In this study, all the participants had to act like they agreed with other people on subjects they really did not agree on. They were also asked to act as if they disagreed with them on matters that actually agreed on.

The scientists referred to these two deceptions as:

1. Ingratiating lies
2. Non-ingratiating lies, respectively

The researchers also had the subjects tell both uningratiating truths and ingratiating truths throughout the study. In the end, it was easier to see the ingratiating lies more than the non-ingratiating ones. The lies were even easier to spot when it was the opposite sex listening to them. Additionally, the more attractive the subject being lied to was, the easier it was to catch on to the lies.

What is funny is the way the lies were spotted. The ingratiating lies were easy to figure out using visual cues such as facial expressions. Meanwhile, lies to the less interesting subject were easier to deduce using auditory cues like vocal tone.

The Mouth versus The Eyes

Many people, when they are faking their feelings, will often let it slip through their eyes. Remember the micro expressions detailed earlier? It is hard to pick up on these, especially because the mouth works hard and effectively at keeping eye movements hidden.

When people are pretending to feel things, the micro expressions will pop up and show their honest feelings, and then right after those micro expressions, the mouth will smile or do something else to hide the real truth of their emotions. The mouth is so effective at hiding the truth that it will often be more than enough to help the eyes escape detection even when the interrogator is focused on the eyes alone. It is simple: People cannot look at eyes without looking at the mouth, and vice versa. Another note to keep in mind: Timing is important. If the smile happens first, it's not masking the eyes. If it comes right after the eyes give off their micro expression, it is masking it. This is why it's not all that easy to figure out lies using just body language and facial expression alone, even when the liar isn't great at lying.

When you cheat, it is easy to forget the morals you hold dear so that you do not have to deal with uncomfortable feelings of cognitive dissonance. In a study titled *Dishonest Deed, Clear Conscience: When Cheating Leads to Moral Disengagement and Motivated Forgetting,* by Shu, Gono, and Bazerman, published in the Personality and Social Psychology Bulletin in 2011, the researchers found that when we cheat or are dishonest, we disengage from our morals and are motivated to forget about whatever concepts of right and wrong we hold dear.

The study showed that the ones who went on to cheat had selectively less memory retention for information that would be deemed morally relevant. Another thing to note is that their memories were no different from those who chose not to cheat before the task began. The difference in memories showed up after. So, cheating made them forget the rules.

Finally, saying to people, "Don't be a liar" works much better than telling them, "Don't lie." Sure, some people get a kick out of cheating, but most people want to do right at the end of the day. Research shows that while people might not mind lying or cheating, no one wants to be labeled a liar or cheater. So, the next time you are dealing with a liar, you can try the "Don't be a liar" statement on them and see if that encourages them to take a few leaps closer to the truth.

Chapter Twelve: Becoming Less Vulnerable

This book wraps up with ways to keep yourself safe and free from the machinations of the Machiavellian. You will learn how to remain impermeable to their antics and be less vulnerable than the average person.

Dealing with Negotiations

How do you deal when you are attacked during a negotiation? Whether you want to call it emotional intelligence or reverse psychology, what you're going to learn right now is something called tactical empathy. This is the weapon you will use to stave off the Machiavellian's attacks. It is anything but the norm. It's very counter-intuitive, but it works. You just need to have the grit to see it through.

First, note the opposite of what the negotiator is upset about. So, what you need to do is simply say, "It seems like you like to . . ." and then end the sentence with the opposite of whatever it is they are whining about. You should be prepared for the spectacle of watching a speeding train come to a complete stop on account of loads of confusion coursing through their mind. How exactly do you pull this off, and what is the reason it works?

The thing is that for every like, there is an equal disciple. If there is something they are coming at you for, you want to go at them for a contrast they value. When you label what they're doing or saying, you're basically triggering their amygdala so that it releases some feel-good dopamine and serotonin. Consider this: If you are dealing with a landlord who does not allow people to sublet their apartments, it means they value stability more than anything. If you're dealing with a landlord who is not open to renegotiations, they obviously think stability is a virtue.

Many objections that come up in the process of negotiation are often founded on uncertainty. You should be the one person keeping a cool head by courageously calling it as you see it. Label the precise fear that they are dealing with. If you really want to get into it, you might want to label it the inverse positive.

Say your neighborhood Mach is attacking something that you really care about or a hot-button issue. Assume that you love to work out, and they say something like, "Working out is incredibly stupid and vain. You're just trying to show you're fitter than I am by doing this workout program." What do you say in response? You could say, "It sounds like you like being with folks who you feel are your equals."

You want to follow up on these labels with a pause. Be silent after that. Allow it to really sink into their noggin and work its way through their body. Do not break the silence first.

You may feel like you don't have the quick wit to label something at the moment, but you do. You only need to practice, and then you will do this naturally. So, just say the words, "It sounds like you like . . ." and wrap up the sentence. Whatever you do, do not turn away from them. Don't speak. Wait. The more you practice doing this, the better you will get at it. Just doing this five times a day for three to four days straight should yield remarkable results. Whenever you're negotiating, keep in mind that you always want to do the counter-intuitive things. This is how you get the upper hand. This labeling technique will land you much better deals than you thought you could get.

The Number One Vulnerability: Thinking You're Too Smart

You might think that you are way too smart to be had by the Machiavellian and other deceptive personalities, but chances are you aren't—and this isn't an insult. You must get rid of that notion because it is exactly what makes you vulnerable to deception. In a book titled *The Confidence Game*, written by Maria Konnikova, there is a lot of information on why people fall for con men and their scams. The con man's victim is not just ignorant and foolish; they're also regular folks who are desperate at that moment or too emotional to see what's really going on.

Most leaders are proud of the fact that they are strategic and logical. Yet Konikova warns that pride is the beginning of the end. Pride blinds you to the Machiavellian's wiles.

The funny thing about past American presidents is that the best ones are humble, while the worst are ineffective and prideful. They were rarely ever open to admitting they were wrong about something, and it was even harder still to own up to their mistakes because they'd had way too much experience—enough to make them think they were above being fallible. However, the great presidents were open, humble, and honest about their weaknesses.

Following this logic, here is a fact that will surprise you: The only other person who can be conned besides the prideful, emotional, or ignorant is the con man himself—as he feels untouchable, immune to ever being stupid enough to fall for a scheme like his. The more you assume you are aware, the easier it is for you to get deeper and deeper into self-deception, which leaves you open to being deceived by other people around you.

Self-Deceit, Denial, and Immunity

There was once a con artist named Fred Demara. He was one of the best the world had ever seen. He had impersonated everyone from businessmen to doctors to priests. During the Korean war, he pretended to be a trauma surgeon aboard a Canadian destroyer. He was able to carry out surgeries just using a manual an actual doctor had written for him.

This same Frank had commissioned a writer to do a biography on him, only to steal the writer's identity. As if things could not get bizarre enough, the biographer whose identity was stolen spent many years later defending him! The people Frank had played for a fool would go the extra mile for him, time after time. The reason for this is that they were not willing to accept that they'd been had—and Frank was well aware of this tendency and exploited it.

Think about this for a minute. Studies by Harvard University and Startup Compass show that not wanting to let a business plan go makes it much less likely that a company will go public. There are too many CEOs and business leaders who do wrong by their employees and their organizations by placing more importance on the appearance of a strong, bulldog leadership, rather than being willing and flexible to go back on their decision or employ a different strategy that can help take their business to groundbreaking heights. The leaders who wind up being fooled are the ones who first fool themselves.

How Not to Be an Idiot

Pride is part of being human. The downside to pride is that it is often lauded as an admirable thing, like taking pride in your work, your abilities, and so on. This is inevitably what opens you up to being deceived—first by yourself and then by others. So, the questions become: How can you avoid this happening? Or how can you not be an idiot?

You must be okay with admitting that you are/might be wrong. In his autobiography, Benjamin Franklin wrote about his decision to start being forthright when he felt he could be wrong as he made his arguments. He noted that since choosing to do this and listening to people he disagreed with rather than waiting to re-emphasize his perception or point of view, he had slashed down his fear of not being right. Here are the man's words so that you can learn from them:

"I made it a rule to forbear all direct contradictions to the sentiments of others and all positive assertion of my own. I even forbade myself the use of every word or expression in the language that imported a fixed opinion, such as 'certainly,' 'undoubtedly,' etc. I adopted instead of them 'I conceive,' 'I apprehend,' or 'I imagine' a thing to be so and so; or 'so it appears to me at present.'

"When another asserted something that I thought an error, I denied myself the pleasure of contradicting him abruptly, and of showing him immediately some absurdity in his proposition. In answering, I began by observing that in certain cases or circumstances, his opinion would be right, but in the present case, there appeared or seemed to be some difference, etc. I soon found the advantage of this change in my approach. The conversations I engaged in went on more pleasantly. The modest way in which I proposed my opinions procured them a readier reception and less contradiction. I had less mortification when I was found to be in the wrong, and I more easily prevailed with others to give up their mistakes and join with me when I happened to be in the right."

You can read Benjamin Franklin's autobiography to learn more about the strategy, which helped the man be much less prideful—or less of an idiot. So, whatever you do, always be open to changing your mind about people, situations, or strategies. Be flexible, and it will be easier for you to notice when you are about to be had. If you're so desperate to have and keep a good reputation, you're going to be a prime target for a Machiavellian. Plus, even after they have had their way with you, you're still going to be self-deluded, refusing to acknowledge you've been taken for a ride. Do not be that person. Don't be an idiot.

Conclusion

You have finally arrived at the end of this book, and the odds are that you have learned a lot about lies, liars, Machiavellians, and their scheming. Never again do you have to allow yourself to become a victim of this set of unscrupulous people.

One other thing to point out is that it is not enough to read one book and assume you do not need to continue to learn about the process of deception. The reason you should continue to educate yourself is simple: Every day, especially with technology and all sorts of innovations coming up, deception is becoming easier and easier to get away with, especially when it comes to the media and political power.

You should go through this book again and mark up sections that stand out. Practice what you have learned so that you become more confident in facing down people who deceive you, or even better, waiting for an opportune time to turn the tables on them and show them to the world for what they really are.

You have done a very smart thing buying this book, and you are even better off for having read it. You do not have to be like the rest of the world—gullible to devious people. You, for once, can take back control of your life. It must be reiterated that the information you have learned within the pages of this book is incredibly potent, and you have to use it responsibly, and preferably, for good.

Never assume for one minute that you are too brilliant to be scammed or deceived. Even the most brilliant minds have been had. You do not have to fall prey to that anymore. If you learn nothing else from this book, keep in mind that you should always be honest and above board in all you do because it serves you better in the long run. At times in this book, the thought might have occurred to you that it would probably serve you to emulate the Machiavellian. The truth is, yes, it will, but only for the short run, and after that, you will have a very difficult time getting people to trust you. You don't want this. So, in everything you do, be honest, open, humble, and remember: Anyone can be a victim. You will not ever be a victim again if you consider that you're not above being deceived.

Here's another book by Neil Morton that you might like

References

http://www.thoughtco.com

http://www.sciencedaily.com

http://www.scientificamerican.com

http://www.theconversation.com

http://www.psychologytoday.com

http://www.time.com

http://www.bustle.com

http://www.theverge.com

http://interestingengineering.com

http://www.howstuffworks.com

http://www.everygirl.com

http://www.lifehacker.com